The Bird Market of Paris

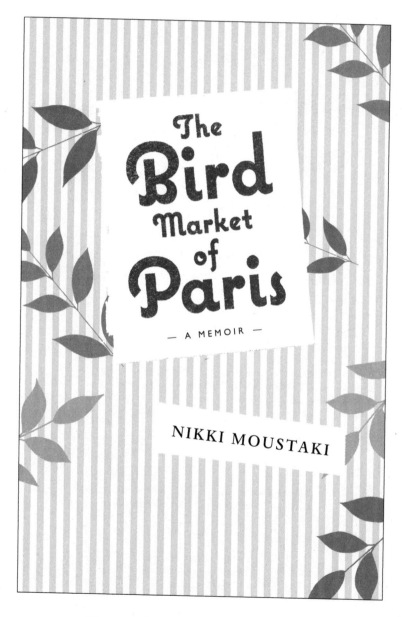

The
Bird
Market
of
Paris

— A MEMOIR —

NIKKI MOUSTAKI

Henry Holt and Company • New York

Henry Holt and Company, LLC
Publishers since 1866
175 Fifth Avenue
New York, New York 10010
www.henryholt.com

Henry Holt® and 🎲® are registered trademarks of
Henry Holt and Company, LLC.

Library of Congress Cataloging-in-Publication Data

Moustaki, Nikki, 1970–
    The bird market of Paris : a memoir / Nikki Moustaki.—First edition.
        pages cm
    ISBN 978-0-8050-9651-4 (hardback)—ISBN 978-0-8050-9652-1 (electronic book)
    1. Moustaki, Nikki, 1970—Childhood and youth.   2. Moustaki, Nikki, 1970—Family.
    3. Moustaki, Nikki, 1970—Travel—France—Paris.   4. Americans—France—Paris—
    Biography.   5. Young women—France—Paris—Biography.   6. Cage birds—France—
    Paris.   7. Markets—France—Paris.   8. Redemption.   9. Alcoholics—United
    States—Biography.   10. Women authors, American—Biography.   I. Title.
    CT275.M673A3 2015
    810.9'9287—dc23   2014012310

Henry Holt books are available for special promotions and
premiums. For details contact: Director, Special Markets.

First Edition 2015

Title page art by Jamie Connel
Bird art courtesy of Pixel 77
Designed by Kelly S. Too

Printed in the United States of America
1   3   5   7   9   10   8   6   4   2

This book is dedicated to my parents,
who indulged me in birds.

"If I could so live and so serve the world that after me there should never again be any birds in cages."

—Isak Dinesen

The Bird Market of Paris

I WOKE ONE AFTERNOON IN NEW YORK CITY, BIRDLESS, HUNGOVER, a yellow screwdriver on the floor next to my dismantled stereo, a debris field of broken glass strewn across the living room floor, not knowing why my gimlet glasses no longer had stems, or why someone had pulverized my turntable into a mound of splintered plastic. What I did know was that I had given away one of the only friends I had left in the world—Jesse, my African Meyer's parrot.

This was the first moment in my life that I didn't have at least one friend with feathers. Birds had filled my world the way blue filled the sky, with a wholeness so natural that an existence without them seemed a perverse impossibility. But alcohol had superseded birds, and my ability to take care of another living creature had died inside a bottle of Malibu rum.

Until that afternoon, birdsong had been the soundtrack of my life. My parents and I had lived close to my grandparents from the time I was very young, and my grandfather, Poppy, kept birds—egg-laying Rhode Island Reds, fancy rolling pigeons, gray cockatiels, yellow ducklings, and gleaming pheasants.

I always believed that my affinity for birds was inherited, or at least contagious. In Corfu, at the end of the nineteenth century, Poppy's father had a white cockatoo that sat on the wall in his courtyard and called each family member by name. Poppy's father passed the "bird gene" to Poppy, who, as an adult, sat in an outdoor table at Café Riche in Cairo, beckoning to the Egyptian sparrow merchants who sold the little birds for food. He would buy several cages of the doomed creatures, fifty to a tiny crate, and as dusk fell over Cairo, Poppy and his only child, my father, would set the birds free from the balcony of their apartment. Poppy passed the bird gene to my father, who was responsible for bringing many of Poppy's birds into our world in South Florida—and for later indulging my bird hobby from beak to tail—effectively passing the bird gene to me.

Ours is not just a love for birds or an appreciation of them, but a particular empathy for anything feathered. I can look at a bird and know what it needs or wants, and I know that Poppy could, too. He taught me how to hypnotize chickens, how to sneak up on flighty pigeons, and how to handle baby birds. I wouldn't call myself a bird whisperer or a bird psychic, because that's not quite right. It's about reading their subtle cues, about paying attention, a kind of avian super intuition.

After receiving a baby lovebird of my own at eighteen years old, I embarked on a feathered journey using my avian genetic inheritance, which eventually led me to a serious avocation in birds—breeding them, rescuing them, and writing about them. That first lovebird taught me what it meant to love a bird, or any creature, unconditionally.

But along the way I discovered alcohol, and it began to consume my life. I was headed toward a featherless existence, leaving that first lovebird and all my other birds behind. While I was at the bottom of my daily martini, Poppy passed away. That loss sent me further into the darkness, into that confused, hungover birdless afternoon, and even further, toward a place without wings.

Until Paris.

Part One

Chapter 1

FROM EARLIEST CHILDHOOD, I WATCHED POPPY'S BIRDS FOR HOURS: the Rhode Island Reds and Japanese silkies, green and golden pheasants, peacocks and peahens, duckling chicks in the spring, rolling pigeons and homing pigeons, star finches and zebra finches, peach-faced lovebirds, gray and white cockatiels, and yellow canaries that sang concertos at dawn and dusk. I thought the pheasants weren't birds at all, but aliens. They were too beautiful to be from this world.

Poppy's chickens were affable birds who let me hold them. There's a photo of me at two years old in diapers in the backyard, trying to ride a big Rhode Island Red. Poppy's pigeons were independent creatures who kept themselves one wing-beat out of my reach. The white pigeons—my favorites—came close when I tossed them the leftovers of our lunch, almost close enough to touch. I'd sit cross-legged in the grass, still as a lighthouse, and wait for them to approach, and then reach out to touch one just as it fluttered from my grasp.

One morning, I discovered a chicken wandering in the yard, long striped feathers trailing from its tail, a gold head and rump,

deep blue wings, and a body as red as cherries. Instead of luring it
with food or talking softly to it, I chased the fast little bird around
the yard for at least half an hour and corralled it into the pigeon
coop, wings flapping, honking and wheezing in fear. Flushed and
breathless, I ran into the house with the "chicken" clutched to my
chest to show Poppy what I had found, so proud of my discovery.

"*Chérie*, you found the new pheasant!" he exclaimed, smiling
and clapping his hands. "*Bravo!*"

For each of my childhood birthdays, Poppy bought me a single white dove, a ritual as regular to us as blowing out candles.
Sometimes the dove arrived in the early morning, and I'd wake
to Poppy standing at my bedside, holding the bird with two
hands, like a sandwich; other birthdays, the dove appeared at
noon in the backseat of Poppy's 1973 ice-blue Ford Pinto, Poppy
having left the house under the guise of purchasing milk, but
returning with a small cardboard box instead, air holes punched
into the top. I counted the days to each birthday dove, a feathered
tick on an invisible calendar marking my growth. Poppy said the
dove ensured I'd have peace for another year.

My earliest, most vivid memory of our tradition is the morning of my eighth birthday. I padded across the terrazzo floor in
bare feet, past my red-eared slider turtle, Sam, who lived in a
Tupperware bowl in the sunny Florida room, past the kitchen
smelling of chocolate and yeast, and my grandmother, whom I
called Nona, laboring there in the heat on my birthday cake. I
swatted open the screen door and found my birthday dove on our
patio, perched in a brass cage dangling from a hook on a curved,
rusted stand. My birthday dove had baby-fine feathers that looked
painted on, a blush-colored beak, and huge, inky, iris-less eyes
surrounded by fleshy white rings. I visited the dove all day, pok-
ing inside the cage to stroke a wing with the tip of my finger.

At dusk, candles blown out and cake eaten, Poppy fished the
dove from the cage and placed its quivering body in my hands.

The bird smelled of musky rain and carnations. I cupped its warm body and trekked into the backyard as sunset painted the sky with pinks and violets, the bird vibrating in my palms like a plucked guitar string.

"Where does my birthday dove go?" I asked. I knew the answer, because I asked the question every year.

"She goes to the heavens, *Chérie*," Poppy said, sweeping his hand over the sky. "And becomes a star to watch over you when I cannot be there myself."

Wanting to do it right, I launched the dove, arms and hands open in a prayer to the sky, tracing its flight with my eyes until the bird swept into the horizon and out of sight. Its wings whistled as it disappeared, and I felt joy mixed with exhilaration, like *I* was made of bird flight.

ONE HUMID WEEKEND MORNING A FEW MONTHS LATER, POPPY ASKED me to help him outside as he passed the kitchen counter, where I was perched on a stool finishing a breakfast of fried potatoes and a bowl of frozen mangos that I ate like Popsicles, the last treasure from our tree's summer harvest.

"Please put on shoes, *Chérie*. I will eat your toes if I see them." Poppy disapproved of my perpetual barefootedness. He was full of stories about rusty nails, gangrene, and amputations.

I crunched over the lawn after him with my sneakers untied, over grass growing stiff and brown in the heat, past the three pomegranate trees, to the coop Poppy had built after the last one rotted into a heap of splintered wood and unraveled wire. He wanted me to duck inside the coop and rescue a baby pigeon that had jumped over a wooden partition and into another nest. The displaced baby's parents had stopped feeding it. The coop's door, an Alice-in-Wonderlandish hatch, did not cooperate with Poppy's adult bones.

I squeezed inside. The enclosure smelled like wet wood and pigeon feces. I associated the musty, almost moldy, odor with the birds and had become as fond of it as someone might of blossoming gardenias. The shelf was partitioned into sections, each one large enough for a pigeon sitting on eggs. Each section had a lip on its outer edge so the eggs wouldn't roll out.

A large squab—a baby pigeon—huddled in the corner of one of the sections, and a small, scrawny squab hunched in the section next to it. Pigeons typically lay two eggs, and as a rule one egg hatches out a male pigeon and the other hatches out a female. The babies have to stay in the nest or the parents won't recognize them—at least, that seemed to be the case with these two squabs.

Poppy stood outside the coop, facing me through the wire.

"*Chérie*, reach up and move the small one into the nest with the fat one," he said, pointing from one pigeon to the other.

One of the adult pigeons scrambled out of a nest and onto a perch above my head. Eggs rolled toward the lip of the partition, glowing white orbs dappled with specks of pigeon poop.

"The baby is starving, *Chérie*, you must move him," Poppy said, pantomiming the gesture of scooping, like dirt in a backhoe.

I reached up, hesitated, pulled my hand back. The baby pigeon looked dangerous: an alien with a huge beak, gray skin, and fluffy greenish moss spreading like disease all over its body.

"Pick him up and move him over," urged Poppy. "Are you afraid? Please do it, *Chérie*."

I wanted to please Poppy, but there was too much activity in the coop. Mature pigeons flapped and cooed in a kind of Morse code, agitated at my intrusion, their chicks begging with high-pitched voices. I gazed at the squab, terror rising, believing I'd suffer serious physical damage if I touched it—maimed fingers or worse.

"He will die," Poppy pleaded. "You can do it. You can rescue him."

I stood on my toes and poised my hand over the baby, ready for pain and the feeling of something sharp, but he was pliable and warm, and I felt his bones slide underneath his skin. He pulled his legs into his body and tensed. I moved him to the proper nest and placed him inside with his sister.

"*Bravo!*" Poppy cheered, clapping his hands. "You saved him!"

I ducked through the coop door into the sunlight as a pair of blue jays dove through the branches of our grapefruit tree. I had changed the path of one creature's future. I felt, for the first time, how fragile everything was, including myself, maybe even Poppy, definitely our birds. That feeling stayed with me long after the baby pigeons feathered out and flew away, long after the coop decayed and Poppy tore it down, long after we moved away from that house and the new owners separated the lot and built two houses on the land that once held birds and wonder.

I SPENT EVERY SUMMER OF MY CHILDHOOD WITH POPPY AND NONA, like grandparent summer camp, but the recession of 1979 forced my parents and me to move into Nona and Poppy's small three-bedroom home in South Miami. Nona and Poppy didn't share the same bed, or even the same room, and they weren't affectionate toward each other, but there was a solidarity between them— the kind of bond, I later realized, that forms between people who have seen things together that they don't want to remember. My parents slept in the third bedroom and I slept with Nona in her bed, which was always filled with birdseed I had dragged under the sheets with my bare feet; I'd wake, a little sweaty, with millet kernels indented into my skin. We didn't have air-conditioning, just the constant whir of fans in every room.

I don't know how my parents felt—that situation couldn't have been comfortable for a married couple—but my transition was seamless. I spent my days watching Poppy seduce birds to eat from his hands and scrutinizing the pita bread in Nona's oven.

"How does the bread fill up with space?" I asked her as I watched the Frisbees of dough puff into inflated globes. I crouched with my nose so close to the oven's window the heat pulsed through me like a melody.

"The bread will fall if you talk about it," Nona whispered, her small, bronze hands white with flour, ready with a flat wooden paddle to rescue the bread. I could match her complexion after a week of beach days; otherwise, I was as pale as my mom, the lone non-Greek in our nuclear family, a native of Coney Island, on the Atlantic, not the Aegean Sea.

"But how does the pocket get into the pita?" I whispered back.

"The dough knows what to do," she said.

I doubted dough had its own volition. I thought Nona didn't want to tell me the secret, because giving it away might jinx the bread, turning it into flat, chewy discs instead of fluffy pockets.

Poppy seemed more willing to let me in on his secrets. Every morning he opened the coop door and released our pigeons. He tossed them birdseed and leftovers from the night before, then turned on the hose and propelled a fine mist through the nozzle, the water effecting a rainbow in the sunlight for the pigeons to bathe beneath. They shifted their heads underneath their wings and writhed their necks at impossible angles. They hunched in the wet grass with wings relaxed, shimmying their bodies deep into the lawn.

Then they bounced up, shook off the bath, and disappeared into the breeze as if they were made of it. There were days when I worried about them being out in the world. Once, driving with Poppy in the afternoon, he pointed out two of our fancy pigeons standing atop a telephone pole. At dusk, the pigeons returned like factory workers and entered the coop, one by one. Poppy often sent me outside to make sure they were all accounted for, all two dozen or so, then I'd close the door and latch it against the raccoons and the occasional fox.

Most evenings, after securing our pigeons, Poppy and I stood in the grass and listened to the mockingbirds and blue jays claiming their territory for the night, the cicadas beginning their loud chorus. Night jasmine filled the air with its heavy syrup. Feet rooted in the earth, I mimicked the mockingbirds to see if they'd call back to me, which made Poppy laugh.

The year we first lived with them, he bought me a pair of blue and white parakeets, Pepito and Pepita, who soon came to a tragic end at the claws of our neighbor's cat. The crime scene was sanitized by suppertime, and a new pair of green parakeets had replaced the unfortunate blue couple. Poppy believed it was a good omen when a pet died in the home—that a tragedy originally intended for humans had taken the animal instead. He said this was why people in the old country kept animals in the yard and house.

Whenever one of my pets passed into the next realm, a canary or a cat, I'd run to Poppy crying, and he'd clap his hands, raise them to the sky, and exclaim, *"Merci, mon Dieu, thanks to God!"* We memorialized the life the animal gave up for us and toasted with apple juice, listing the animal's positive attributes: *Henry was a fine duck, a friendly and beautiful duck, with the prettiest feathers, whose honk could be heard down the block.*

Nona was a gracious and proper woman, but had some old world superstitions that I couldn't understand. She didn't allow me to keep the seashells I collected on the beach. She said they were bad luck because they were dead, and you don't bring death into the house.

She said that when someone shattered a dish or a glass, it meant something evil had been put upon them, but now the spell was broken. She burned frankincense, myrrh, and mastic every few days, carrying the little dish of burning sap all over the house to drive out evil that may have settled in the corners.

She wore "evil eye" amulets, royal blue glass discs with concentric white, light blue, and black circles in the center: one around her neck, one in a ring, and one on a bracelet, and kept them all over the house, saying they repelled other people's evil thoughts about you.

When I was ten years old, Nona asked, "Who do you love more, me or Poppy?" How much Nona's eyes looked like mine, in shape and color, deep brown with flecks of gold. I loved both Nona and Poppy, but if the scales tipped, they tipped a feather's weight in Poppy's favor. I forced my face into as neutral a position as possible. Nona said, "I knew it. You love your grandfather more."

Poppy pulled silver dollars from people's ears and gave the coins to them. He looked people in the eye. He believed in giving small presents to everyone, from local celebrities to the receptionist at his dentist's office, and he held lunch parties at his fashion design studio where he plied his clients with homemade spanakopita and baklava. I helped him hard-boil eggs in tea so they were brown instead of white. Nothing in Poppy's world could be ordinary.

He was a gifted raconteur, telling stories over and over, each time adding another tiny detail, embellishments like sequins on a dress. He talked a bit about Egypt, about the green talking parrots that lived in the palace and about the superior nature of Cairo's fruit and vegetables, but most of all, Poppy overflowed with stories about Paris, the city's broad sidewalks where ten people could walk shoulder to shoulder, and the lazy afternoons sitting in cafés, people watching. Rarely did I hear about the Pyramids of Giza or the Sphinx. He was taken with Paris, and through his stories I was taken with it, too. He said he would take me there someday.

He told me about the Marché aux Oiseaux, the bird market of Paris, held on Sundays in conjunction with the famous flower market and close to Notre Dame. I heard about the bird market of Paris from Poppy so often, it became something I had to experience.

"You can hear the music of the birds a mile away," he told me. "The birds are a miracle, you cannot imagine such beautiful birds, the colors, the songs." He spoke emphatically, like a man running for office, and I believed him.

In my imagination, birdsong filled the market, waving and swelling like smoke, sunlight bathing each feather to a glisten, down to the shaft where the feather anchors into the wing. Pullets, canaries, and finches playing with the afternoon light, an iridescent sheen bouncing from their tightly groomed feathers. Roosters with feathers on their feet. Pigeons with tails spreading up and out like an Andalusian lady's fan. I didn't know these birds, but Poppy's talk made them irresistible. *That's the way I'll love them, too*, I thought, *when I'm old enough to go to Paris*. It was as inevitable as the stars, which were birds, after all.

Chapter 2

POPPY CUT HIS SHOULDER-LENGTH, FLOWING SILVER HAIR HIMSELF by looking at the back of his head in a mirror. He had a strong, straight nose, and was known for his overgrown eyebrows; he'd roll them upward into curls, like handlebar mustaches on the outside edges of his eyes, and chase me around the house or yard as I squealed, pretending to be afraid. He seemed tall when I was a child, but he was of average height. I rode on his broad shoulders to pick grapefruit and key limes from the taller branches on the trees in our yard.

Most close friends and relatives called Poppy by our last name, Moustaki, including Nona, though when I was around, she called him Poppy. My father, his son, called him Monsieur Moustaki. My mom called him by his first name, Soli, and acquaintances and business associates called him Bruno, his middle name.

Though my family was Greek, they didn't speak Greek because they originated in Corfu, a tiny Grecian island with its own many dialects, and they were Jews. Poppy's parents spoke Italkian, a mixture of Hebrew and Italian sprinkled with enough Greek so that invading armies over the centuries couldn't understand them.

Poppy's father, Victorio, a tailor, and his mother, Stella, fled Corfu to Egypt in 1891 after a period of civil unrest, when most of the Jews were forced off the island. In 1917, they brought Poppy into the world in Cairo, then a metropolitan city bustling with Europeans who spoke French as a common language, and who, with a liberal measure of Arabic, could also communicate with the Egyptians. With an ear for languages, Poppy learned Greek and became fluent in ten other languages: Italkian, French, Arabic, Hebrew, English, Italian, Portuguese, German, Spanish, and later, in Miami, Haitian Creole. He defined fluency as the ability to speak about philosophy in the language. He spoke English well, but never used contractions.

My father, Poppy and Nona's only child, was born in 1943 in Heliopolis, Egypt, a home birth at 39 Alexandria Street. He learned only French and Arabic as a child. Despite the religious differences, he was educated by Jesuits in a French-speaking Catholic school in Cairo because Nona felt it was the best school in the city.

Poppy had learned to sew in his father's tailor shop, but worked as a military attaché in communications during World War II in the Greek army. He was the liaison officer for the British army under General Montgomery—and, later, the liaison between the Greek and British armies and the Free French army. He hinted that he had also been a spy for the British, rooting out Nazis hiding in Cairo.

After the war, Poppy became a couture dressmaker, designing gowns for rich and famous ladies in Cairo, including King Farouk's wife and small daughters, and the king's sister, Princess Fawzia Fuad, wife of the Shah of Iran.

Poppy's stories about Cairo sounded glamorous—yachting, car races, servants, parties. Photos of Nona as a young woman show her dressed in slinky sequined dresses, posing with the king's court at parties, Poppy at her side. King Farouk became a main character in Poppy's tales of Egypt: how Poppy played backgammon tournaments with the king and wouldn't lose games on purpose, though most other people were afraid to win against His Majesty; how the king cheated at poker—if he had three kings in his hand, he'd consider himself the fourth king and win; and how the king would eat "twenty-four pigeon soup," made from slow-boiling twenty-four pigeons into a small bowl of rich broth.

In 1952, Gamal Abdel Nasser overthrew King Farouk in a bloody revolution, and thousands of Europeans and Jews left Egypt at gunpoint, taking only what they could carry. The revolutionaries killed many who refused to go, including Nona and Poppy's friends and neighbors. The dissidents burned the blocks around my grandparents' home—every office building, every store, every nightclub, and every restaurant. Nona and Poppy watched the mob wash through the streets toward their apartment to steal guns in the hunting club at the bottom of the building. Nona, Poppy, and my nine-year-old father ran down the emergency staircase and through a side exit as the furious riot breached the front door.

They fled down an alleyway and saw a taxi sitting there, as if it had been waiting for them—a cosmic cab with the door wide open. They told the driver to take them to Heliopolis, where Nona's mother lived. Poppy had managed to grab a few rare coins, and Nona had filled her pockets with the contents of her jewelry box. They had nothing else but the clothes they were wearing.

My father watched people drench cats in gasoline and set them on fire—the cats bolted in flames into buildings and set Cairo ablaze—and saw people jump from the tops of burning buildings into Tahrir Square. Dissidents surrounded the cab in a swarm of fists and rage as the driver honked and urged the mob to part for the car, gunning the engine a few feet at a time for miles, swallowed by a mass of humans, crying for freedom from the king's reign, spurred by indignation that they were being led by a Turk, not an Arab, and a lover of foreigners and foreign things. Poppy's impeccable Arabic allowed my family to survive. The police stopped the cab many times, the dissident crowd rocking the car back and forth, trying to overturn it, and Poppy retorting in Arabic with "Hey, get out of our way! I am one of you!"

They returned to Cairo a few weeks later to find their apartment ransacked and burned, but they remained in Egypt another four years under Nasser's regime, where one word against the government made a person disappear. During the violent conflict in 1956 for control of the Suez Canal, Poppy and Nona sat under heavy blankets each afternoon listening to a barely audible shortwave radio—it was illegal to tune in to foreign stations, and the punishment for doing so was death. They waited for French radio to announce where the evening's French and British aerial bombardment of Cairo would take place so they could stay at a friend's house in a different neighborhood if the bombs were scheduled nearby. At sundown, before bombing commenced, police roamed the streets screaming, in Arabic, "Jew, son of a dog, shut out the lights."

The police placed Poppy under house arrest with the rest of the foreigners. My father's school was turned into a prison camp. Every male non-Arab over eighteen was detained there, his head shaved, his street clothing swapped for a blue jumpsuit. Poppy escaped internment because he had a friend in the district attorney's office. In late 1956, Poppy, Nona, and my father were stripped of their belongings and placed onto a boat bound for Europe. Crossing the gangway, Nona was ordered to surrender her wedding ring; Nasser's military personnel wanted to make sure the refugees left with nothing. Nona stood tall—all five feet of her—looked the soldier in the eye, and said, "Over my dead body." He waved her onto the ship.

Nona, Poppy, and my father had a cabin, but many others didn't, nor did they have blankets, and people froze to death on the deck. They arrived in the port of Zeebrugge, Belgium, traveled by train to Paris, and struggled to survive in their new city, sometimes sharing one potato among the three of them as an evening meal. Nona often gave her share of potato to my father, stifling her own hunger by drinking hot water. Poppy was resourceful—and a good gambler—earning money playing backgammon tournaments. They spent four years in Paris. My father attended Parisian schools, and Poppy started sewing again, designing dresses for socialites, including Charles de Gaulle's brother's wife and daughters.

Just after the war, Nona's sister had married an American pilot who flew private jets for Saudi Arabian king Ibn Saud, and the pilot sponsored Nona, Poppy, and my father to come to the United States, three of the two thousand visas issued by Senator Jacob Javitz of New York for Egyptian refugees. My dad remembers the ship pulling into New York Harbor on a cold day in January, after a rough, seasick, transatlantic journey from Europe when he was thirteen, gazing at the Statue of Liberty with her flame igniting the sky. He spoke one word of English: *milk*.

After the family moved to Miami, Poppy opened his design studio downtown not far from the famous Coppertone billboard featuring a little suntanned girl and a black puppy pulling down her bathing suit bottom to reveal her tan line. Poppy ascended into the top ranks of the local fashion designers in the mid-1960s. He became somewhat of a celebrity, appearing on *The Dick Cavett Show*, *The Jackie Mason Show*, and *The Merv Griffin Show*.

Every Christmas, Poppy decorated a giant evergreen for Miami's courthouse with heart-shaped ornaments dotting the tree like hibiscus and pairs of live doves in gold cages embedded into its branches. On the tree's top, a sparkling flocked dove with outstretched wings readied itself for flight, holier than any angel.

I DON'T THINK POPPY SAW MUCH OF MY FATHER WHILE HE WAS building his couture business in Paris, and then again in Miami, so when I came along, it was a chance for him to "raise" another child.

He would open his wallet and ask people, "Do you want to see a picture of my pride and joy?" They would nod, and he'd show them a wallet-size photograph of the furniture wax Pride and the dish soap Joy, both sitting in front of a blue photo backdrop as if they went to Sears to have their portrait taken. After the laughter, he'd turn to a photo of me and say, "That is my little girl." Most people assumed that I was his daughter.

Both of my parents worked long hours, first in the garment business and then in luxury car sales, so Poppy took me everywhere with him: to the ballet, classical concerts, and the racetrack. I thought everyone's grandfather took them to grown-up parties to meet the mayor. I accompanied Poppy to events with the who's who of Miami and beyond. Walter Cronkite said he liked my curly hair, and Dionne Warwick asked me if I wanted to sing when I grew up—of course I did, but I couldn't carry a tune in a basket. I met Count Basie and scored autographs from the ballet dancers Rudolf Nureyev and Mikhail Baryshnikov. Poppy had dined with everyone from kings to congressmen, from Pavarotti to the Grand Imperial Wizard of the Ku Klux Klan—he used to show me the man's business card and laugh. My childhood was full of celebrities I didn't recognize, and rail-thin models with jutting clavicles pinching my cheeks and painting lipstick on me at fashion shows.

Poppy sewed dresses of flowing, colorful jersey, embellished with gold rope and dyed feathers, and he invented a dress called the "M" that could be worn a hundred different ways, his trademark design in Miami in the 1970s. He created miniature versions of his dresses for me, and I walked the runway by myself at the opening of his lavish fashion shows at the Doral, the Biltmore, and various country clubs, tossing rose petals onto the runway from a wicker basket. The spotlights in my eyes blurred the audience into a black mass, a huge, dark lake that issued a collective gasp—the sound most people make at a basketful of puppies— as I stepped from behind the curtain and minced to the end of the catwalk, smiling and terrified, tossing each petal for Poppy, taking each step as if it were the most important step of my life. I was a shy, bookish, frizzy-headed imp with deep-set eyes and cowlicks at my hairline that formed my bangs into a heart shape on my forehead, but in those few minutes, I was a model.

Poppy hung my finger paintings and drawings all over his studio and showed them to everyone who came through the door as if I were Picasso himself. We spent long beach days together at Crandon Park, where he gave me paddleball lessons at the edge of the surf as seagulls screeched like faulty brakes and plunged at our blanket to steal my potato chips. He indulged me with hot fudge sundaes and bought me an encyclopedia volume every month for two years until I had the entire set. The books had faux leather bindings, and each page was edged with gold, so when the book closed the fore edge gleamed like treasure.

Chapter 3

THE YEAR I TURNED NINE, MY PARENTS OFFERED TO TAKE ME TO Walt Disney World a month after my birthday instead of having a birthday party. Maybe it was a kindness because I didn't have enough friends to warrant an ice cream cake and bouncy house. But the lack of a party dogged me, and I couldn't sleep till well past midnight the night before my birthday. Nona snored in bed beside me as I plotted a party for myself.

On my birthday, my parents had to work late selling cars at their respective car dealerships—Ferraris for my dad and Subarus for my mom—so I was alone with Nona and Poppy that afternoon and had just over an hour to prepare.

I had invited four girls from school to arrive for my party at four o'clock. I didn't use invitations bought from a stationery store like the invites other kids dispensed for their parties: card-stock status symbols insinuating the scrumptiousness of the cake and the bounty of the take-away party favor bag. I wrote the invites on lined paper and decorated them with Magic Markers—hearts, flowers, and swirled flourishes in each corner—and passed them to the girls at lunch.

Nona baked my favorite coffee-flavored cake, ten thin layers, including two layers of hardened caramelized sugar and chocolate icing with a little rum in it. She drove me in her blue weather-worn 1965 Plymouth Valiant, which didn't have air-conditioning, to the five-and-dime where I bought party favors for my guests: a fuzzy bunny statuette, yellow plastic sunglasses, a small green plastic tub shaped like a trash can containing green slime with eyeballs in it, a Strawberry Shortcake doll knockoff, four packs of cherry Pop Rocks, and a small stuffed puppy dog.

At home, I spent half an hour layering the prizes with tissue paper, wrapping paper, and tape, so we could play my favorite party game where we sat in a circle and passed the wrapped present around as someone played music in the background. When the music stopped, whoever held the present peeled one of the layers of wrapping. The person to peel off the last ply of paper kept the present.

I slipped on a dress emblazoned with a pattern of cherries and a bright green sash at the waist, the full skirt whooshing over my thighs with a thin layer of scratchy crinoline beneath it. Poppy had designed and sewn the dress for my birthday after I chose the fabric from the hundreds of bolts of cotton in his design studio. I loved caressing the exotic fabrics, holding the eyelet to the light, swathing myself in the soft jersey and charmeuse, and inhaling the scent of the rough muslin, a fragrance like milk and popcorn, when Poppy ironed it.

It was warm for October, and we had multiple fans whirling as I played Michael Jackson's *Off the Wall* record on the turntable, an album I had been wearing out since summer. The mellow groove of "Rock with You" mingled with the yeasty smell of baking bread. I yearned for pink party streamers and a "Happy Birthday" banner, like the one I'd had the year before, but it was too late for that.

Four o'clock came—no guests. I called one girl and she said her mother wouldn't let her come. At five thirty, another girl called to decline the invitation. I didn't have the other girls' phone numbers, so I asked Nona to look them up in the white pages. Nona said if they didn't want to come, I shouldn't chase them.

She brought me the latch hook rug I'd been working on and told me to add more yarn while I waited for my guests. Nona was gifted at arts and crafts, skilled at stained glass, and could sew almost as well as Poppy.

Poppy often took me to visit Nona at Miami's National Parkinson's Institute, where she worked as an assistant physical therapist, and I'd help her create arts and crafts projects with the Parkinson's patients, finger painting and cutting out paper flowers, helping their trembling hands use the blunt scissors.

But that evening I didn't have the patience to work on the place-mat-size rug, which, when finished, would depict an alert-looking owl perched on a pine bough.

I put down the latch hook and yarn and sat at the window, staring at cars cruising down our quiet street. I leapt to my feet each time one approached, but each time the car drove by. Around six o'clock, Nona dragged me from the window and asked me to show her the game I had intended to play with my guests. I didn't want to play yet, in case the girls arrived, but by six thirty, she was sitting on the orange shag carpet with me while Poppy manned the record player, and we passed gifts back and forth to choppy versions of "Don't Stop Till You Get Enough" and "Off the Wall" until one of us found the present underneath the layers of wrapping. Nona pretended to be delighted and surprised at the gift when she won, turning it over in her hands to study it, as if she had never seen it and hadn't bought it a couple hours before. I held back one present in case the girls showed up.

Nona pressed candles into the rummy cake and lit them. She

and Poppy sang the "Happy Birthday" song off-key as she walked toward me, balancing the tall cake in both hands. How could I blow out the candles without at least my parents there?

"Make a wish, Nicole," Nona said, smiling, placing the cake on the Formica coffee table in front of me. There were ten candles—nine for my age and one "for good measure." I tried not to cry as I turned my back on the cake and returned to my station at the window.

"You must blow out your candles," Poppy said.

"Not now, please."

"Why do you wait like this, *Chérie*?" His voice was sympathetic, like he was consoling a sick person.

"It's not my birthday until everyone's here."

"The candles are melting on your cake," Poppy said. "Can we have cake now and then we will all sing to you again when your mommy and daddy come home?"

A car turned onto our street. I stood on the couch for a better view as it drove out of sight. I glanced over my shoulder—Nona was carrying the flaming cake back to the kitchen, blowing out the candles one by one, smoke trailing her like a car burning oil.

Poppy sat beside me, the sun a memory beyond our rooftop, high cirrus clouds changing from white to fuchsia and gold.

"It is time for your dove." He placed his hand on my shoulder, and I wanted to tell him that staring at the street would bring my parents home sooner, but I didn't want to jinx it by revealing the secret.

Poppy wanted us to release my birthday dove into the twilight, but that would signal my birthday ending and another year beginning, and my parents still weren't there. Nona spoke to her sister on the phone behind me in French, saying "the poor little one," and tsking with her tongue.

"Not until they come home."

"*Chérie*, if we do not set your dove free while there is still light in the sky, how will she find her way in the darkness?" He sat next to me and smoothed my frizzy hair.

I thought about that for a minute and followed him to the patio.

With the warm dove in my hands, I forgot about the window. I felt glorious and somehow holy, rising above the problems of my new nine-year-old world. I watched the dove ascend from my grasp, stutter in the air for a moment, then right itself and dive into the dusk, aiming for the moon.

We waved swarms of buzzing gnats away from our ears, silent together, until the first stars appeared. Before I could ask Poppy where my birthday dove went after she left my hands, he pointed to a patch of sky and said, "See that star? She is yours."

The sky grew from plum to the color of crows, and I moved back to my perch at the window to wait for my parents. Disembodied headlights cruised down our block, and every time a quartz-halogen flash appeared, I would turn to the empty space behind me and yell, "They're home!" But it was never them. My arms tingled and grew numb, but I wouldn't leave the window.

"*La Petite*, come have a snack," Nona said. She always called me *La Petite*, as Poppy called me *Chérie*.

"What time was I born?" I asked her.

She studied my face as if I were a chalkboard scribbled over with a complex physics formula. "Why do you want to know?"

"Because it's not my birthday until the time I was born, so if they come home before then, they won't miss my birthday."

She contemplated me, then kissed my head and walked away. Again, I heard angry French whispers behind me, something about my parents and "the poor little one."

"I understand you," I said without turning around. I couldn't speak French, but I had good comprehension for simple conversations. They switched to speaking Arabic. I understood one phrase in the entire language: *bukra fil mish-mish*—when the apricots bloom—the Arabic version of our less delicate maxim "when pigs fly."

Nona returned with a provolone sandwich and a cup of lentil soup, and I ate both, glaring into the darkness, wishing for cat vision and a magic wand.

When I finished eating, Nona brought me a wrapped box, bigger than anything I had received for any birthday, and said it was from her and Poppy. I couldn't believe how huge the box was, and it distracted me from the blankness outside. The box had to contain something great. I peeled the tape from the top of the box as Nona and Poppy stood over me.

"Rip it, *Chérie*," Poppy urged. But I wasn't the ripping paper kind of kid. I was a saver. I peeled the tape until the paper fell away to reveal a big blue globe, the curves of its body breaching the colorful box through circular openings on four sides, as if the globe wanted to force its way out of the packaging.

"This is so you can see the world," Nona said.

With Poppy's help, I removed the globe from the box and placed it on the coffee table. He spun the globe on its tilted axis.

"Here is Egypt," he said, fingering a purple country tattooed with the blue Nile, a snake winding through the desert, forming a shape like a distended stomach with an outie belly button. "You see, here, Heliopolis, where your daddy was born, and Cairo, where we lived. *Chérie*, now you find Greece."

I peered around Europe and turned the globe, but Poppy put his hand on mine. He placed his finger below an orange country and a group of orange islands speckling the turquoise sea.

"Show her Corfu," Nona said.

Poppy's finger roamed up the coast of Greece. "There is no Corfu."

"No Corfu!" Nona exclaimed. "What did they do with Corfu?"

"They omitted it," Poppy said, peering at the spot where Corfu should have been, surrounded by the blue waters of the Ionian Sea.

"What kind of world doesn't have Corfu?"

"It must still be there. We would have seen on the news if it sank into the sea."

Nona tsked with her tongue and walked into the kitchen, her clear plastic flip-flops *ca-chuck ca-chucking* with each step. Poppy's finger traveled again, tracing the forty-five-degree line of longitude, and landed on a green country.

"Look here, *Chérie*." I squinted at the globe as he tapped on a small black star in northern France. "Paris. The best city in the world. We will go there someday together."

I pulled the globe into my lap and spun it, tracing my finger over bumpy mountain ranges, outlining continents, traversing oceans in seconds. I inspected Paris, then Miami. I wished I were in Paris, away from this birthday failure. I glanced at the time on Poppy's watch. Almost nine o'clock.

"What time was I born?" I asked Poppy.

He smoothed my hair again. "I do not know, *Chérie*. That is a good question. Ask your mommy when she comes home."

I hoped I wasn't born until just before midnight. That would give my parents time to arrive before my birthday ended. I set the globe aside, turned back to the window, and glared into the darkness.

At ten o'clock, Nona brought me a slice of birthday cake. It had a hole in the top where a candle had been. I ate it slowly, face framed inside the window. Passing strangers would see a girl eating cake, and I wondered if they'd know it was my birthday.

By half past ten, Nona and Poppy had convinced me to change into my nightclothes, brush my teeth, and try to sleep. They said I would hear when my parents arrived. Nona sat on our queen-size bed and we ate cherry Pop Rocks, giggling like two girls at a slumber party at how the candy sizzled on our tongues. She kissed me good night and shut the door behind her. We didn't always go to bed at the same time.

"See you tomorrow!" I trilled after her, as I did every night, feeling that if she didn't say it back she might die in her sleep. I saved her with this ritual each evening, though she didn't know it. I'd badger her if she didn't say it back, trailing behind her with my blue security blanket, BaaBaa, dragging on the floor until she relented, said the magic phrase, and ferried me back to bed.

"See you tomorrow," Nona replied, voice muffled through the door.

Crickets and cicadas serenaded one another over our lawn, an unrelenting wall of sound mingled with the soft whoosh of the areca palm's fronds teasing the breeze outside my window. Passing cars didn't stop, one after another, at what seemed like regular intervals, shining their lights between the cracks in my curtains, slinging shadows around the room like a magician throwing cards into a hat. I held the last wrapped party favor, squishing the paper around the surprise gift. I knew the contents by process of elimination, but this last present gave me hope. My birthday wasn't over. It wasn't midnight, was it?

I unwrapped one layer of the party favor gift and set aside the crumpled paper. Then I peeled another layer. If I peeled slowly enough, I'd hear a car engine whine into the driveway. Peel. It would stop and I'd hear two car doors open, then slam shut. Peel. Then footsteps toward the front door. Peel. Keys in the front door. Peel. Door open with a squeak. Peel. Door shut. Peel. Parents walking to my room. Peel. The door opening. Peel. A yellow triangle of light shafting onto the floor toward my bed. Peel. "Happy birthday!" Peel.

Then it was in my hands, a fuzzy bunny statuette. I couldn't see it in the darkness, but I could feel its velvety ears and smooth nose. I raised it to my face and rubbed it along my cheek, then scrunched into my pillow and pulled the sheet over my head, crunchy, rumpled paper falling onto the floor. I wedged the bunny into the crook of my neck, where I found it in the morning.

I smelled Nona's breakfast through the crack in the door: potatoes and sardines frying, *koulourakia portokaliou*, my favorite orange-flavored cookies, baking in the stove with fresh pita bread, and the slimy but delicious green *molokhia* soup already boiling for lunch. I winced at the sun through a sliver in the yellow curtains and wondered if my birthday dove was safe. For the first time in all my birthdays I regretted releasing her. It might have been the first time I felt regret at all. I didn't feel nine. I felt endless, like I filled all the space in the universe, and like I took up no space at all.

Chapter 4

WHEN I WAS THIRTEEN AND IN SEVENTH GRADE, MY PARENTS AND I moved from Nona and Poppy's home to our own house in Coconut Grove on Royal Palm Avenue. The house was set back from the street, shaded by wild trees no gardener ever tended, with a colossal banyan tree in the front that had to be a hundred years old, its gangly roots reaching for the ground like Rapunzel's penny-colored mane. I'd braid the roots and swing over the pebbled driveway like Tarzan. A sinkhole on the property filled with rainwater during storms, and I'd toss pebbles into the mysterious chasm, wondering how deep it went, and if it would someday swallow the house. I had my own room, and I snuck into the neighbor's yard to swim in their pool when they weren't home. I liked our new digs, but Poppy had to drive nearly an hour in traffic to pick me up for weekends with him and Nona.

"Does your daddy ever smoke funny cigarettes?" Poppy asked me one day as he drove me west in his silver Honda hatchback.

My dad was a five-pack-a-day Marlboro Red chain-smoker. He always had a cigarette in his hand, even in photographs from before I was born. Nicotine perfumed every crevice of the house, cleaved to the back of every breath. I was probably a pack-a-day smoker from secondhand smoke.

Nona had smoked for forty years, too, a constant cloud of cigarette fumes anointing her head like a nicotinic halo, but she quit in her sixties, then sat on the couch every day after she retired watching *Days of Our Lives* and *General Hospital*, cracking sunflower seeds. Instead of ashtrays overflowing with cigarette butts all over the house, they overflowed with a deluge of crunchy black shells.

But Poppy was referring to the thin rolled cigarettes my dad and some of his friends smoked. These were the cigarettes blowing by me at dinner parties, passed from adult to adult, a tiny Olympic torch with a hypnotic burning ember at the tip.

"Funny cigarette" plants grew in our backyard and on our roof in a homemade greenhouse built with pine stakes and opaque plastic panels. On sunny afternoons, when the western sun hit the panels, the dark silhouettes of dozens of plants shimmied in the breeze, like a crowd of people with hundreds of flickering hands. My dad had been cultivating a healthy urban "funny cigarette" farm for years. He called them his "tomato plants," though they never bore any tomatoes. Sometimes he'd have me turn on the faucet outside that propelled water through the irrigation system to the plants on the roof. They grew taller than I was, wild and pretty, the color of a praying mantis. My dad would harvest the plants and leave the crop in sticky, fragrant piles drying all over the house on oilcloth tarps. My parents had been batik-wearing, daisy-carrying hippies in the 1960s; of course there were "funny cigarettes" around.

"You have never seen any funny cigarettes?" Poppy asked again. "What about your daddy's friends, do they smoke funny cigarettes?"

Saying *yes* would ignite an investigation. I insisted I didn't know anything about the funny cigarettes.

My dad was a manager at the Ferrari and Porsche Collection in Miami, and my mom sold cars at the Subaru and Saab Collection. This was the 1980s, when every other car on the Miami streets was a shiny, expensive import.

My mom or dad picked me up from junior high every day in a different fancy car belonging to one of their dealerships. Every afternoon, boys from school waited outside the building to see what make and model of car would roll up. Maybe today it would be a Rolls-Royce Silver Cloud, a Porsche 911, or a Ferrari Mondial. I had the reputation of being a drug dealer's kid. I knew a few kids whose parents *were* drug dealers, children of people who bought cars from my dad, kids I had playdates with on weekends. They had tigers and bubbly Jacuzzis and waterfalls cascading into their giant pools and projection TVs in their mammoth living rooms. The closest I had to a tiger was Sylvester, the black and white stray kitten I had plucked from a box in front of Publix. We didn't have a projection TV. We didn't even have a bathtub.

My parents entertained guests several times a week, someone from the Ferrari dealership, or patrons from a local bar, the Taurus, where my parents often drank after work. They took me to the Taurus with them, but they wouldn't let me sit at the bar, a seat I desperately wanted. The bar was the nexus of activity, bordered by a hedgerow of mysterious off-limits bottles handled by a man of authority, who plucked them with confidence from their seats in front of a backlit mirror. People entreated the guardian of the bottles to give them a small portion of the liquid contents, some of which smelled of oranges, chocolate, or licorice. I wanted to taste them all. Instead, I'd end up in a back room playing Ms. Pac-Man for hours at a cocktail sit-down machine opposite one of my dad's friends, the folksinger Fred Neil, who wrote "Everybody's Talkin'," the theme song for the film *Midnight Cowboy*.

I liked my dad's work friends—like Louie, the good-natured Cuban car salesman who had three daughters around my age whom I played with when we vacationed together in Marco Island, on Florida's west coast—but I resented my parents' bar friends, the men I called the "couch drunks." They'd sleep on our couch for months at a time and keep my parents up all night drinking, and they'd be there in the morning as I padded to the bathroom to brush my teeth. One of them drank my dad's cologne.

My parents collected down-on-their-luck drunks the way some people collect dogs from the pound—they felt sorry for these people, who didn't have homes or bright prospects. But the couch drunks took attention away from me, and my parents bought them drinks with money I thought would be better spent on fashionable shoes for me so the kids at school wouldn't put gum in my hair anymore. The couch drunks were down on their luck through every fault of their own, it appeared, but they amused my parents, whose bustling social circle was open to the Ferrari contingent, the hardworking rank and file, *and* the down-and-out, as long as the people were witty, intelligent, and told great stories. The couch drunks were always gracious to me, extending themselves as friends, but I was suspicious of anyone who seemed to be scamming my parents and keeping them out all night. After a few weeks or a year, each couch drunk would move on to drunker pastures, and another would take his place.

"Uncle Fitch," who slept on our couch off and on, was a purveyor of funny cigarettes, among other substances. He was scruffy, with a huge handlebar mustache, and spoke in a growling baritone, as if he had gargled with nails. Uncle Fitch had a mean aura that wavered around him like heat waves on asphalt in summer. He told stories about deadly bar fights and drug smuggling that entertained my dad as they drank together.

"Little girl, get me a beer!" was Uncle Fitch's battle cry as he pointed to the fridge, snapping his fingers. I'd race to the kitchen, grab a green glass bottle of St. Pauli Girl, and ferry it to him.

"Not cold enough," he'd contend, and snap those nicotine-stained fingers again, handing the beer back to me. "And get your father one, too."

Uncle Fitch left our couch after a year and moved in with a woman he'd met at the Taurus. We visited him at a little house in the middle of an avocado grove at the end of a long gravel drive-way. Avocado trees whispered in the darkness. The naked yellow porch light, drowning in moths, was the one spark in a chasm of pitch and sighing leaves on either side of us.

Fitch was ensconced in a La-Z-Boy recliner, a walking cane leaning on the chair, an empty beer in front of him. He had mouthed off to a group of teenagers at Haulover Beach and they'd beaten him with baseball bats, putting him in the hospital for weeks.

"Hey, hey!" Fitch bellowed. "Come on in."

A dark-haired, mousy woman with an expressionless face appeared in the kitchen doorway and Fitch introduced her to us as if she were a piece of furniture. "Get us some beers, woman," he ordered. She disappeared.

"Kids, come here," Fitch spat, and two skinny, dark-haired kids appeared, a girl and a boy, perhaps twelve and ten years old. He introduced them as the woman's kids. They stood close together, four feet away from Fitch, arms at their sides like sol-diers, staring at the floor. Fitch snapped his fingers and pointed at his shoe.

"Get on your knees and tighten my laces," he said. The little boy dove at Fitch's right shoe. The boy didn't look up at Fitch, just untied both of his shoes and retied them. Fitch didn't like the way the boy had tied one of his shoes, and ordered that he tie it again.

"You see," Fitch said, "I have them all in line."

I pitied those kids. I imagined their terrified life with Uncle Fitch, and I was glad it wasn't mine. Later, Fitch was sent to jail for attempted murder of the kids' mother. He had shot at her with a rifle as she ran from him through the avocado grove, bullets hitting only trees. In my early twenties, my dad told me that Fitch had died homeless on a mattress in an abandoned building, an empty bottle of scotch and a bottle of painkillers near his head. I felt sad for him, but kind of relieved for the world.

POPPY HATED THE COUCH DRUNKS. "THAT BLOODY SYCAMORE," HE'D hiss under his breath when he encountered one of them. "Bloody sycamore" was Poppy's favorite substitute curse phrase. He was as dry of expletives as he was of alcohol, at least in a language I understood; he cursed liberally in Arabic when someone cut him off on the road.

He said to me, many times, finger pointing to the sky in a kind of oath, "*Chérie*, I never took a drink in my life." He loathed taking pills, too, in practice and as a concept, and called people who took pills—even prescription pills—"pillographers." He thought doctors were out to poison people.

"Do you know the root of the word *poison*?" he'd ask. I'd shake my head, though he had told me the answer a million and one times. "*Pharmakeia*. Stemming from the Greek. In English, it is where we get the word *pharmacy*."

During my childhood, Poppy and I often spent Saturdays together at the Surf Club on Miami Beach, where Poppy played in an ongoing backgammon tournament. The Surf Club had a saltwater pool with a high diving board, and two tame capuchin monkeys who swung down from the banyan trees to snatch French fries from my plate. Poppy pointed out an old lady at the bar, an ancient, wrinkled socialite sitting by herself, head bobbing and teeth clenching, and whispered, "She took a lot of drinks, and look what happened to her."

He greeted the frail woman, called her *mademoiselle* and

kissed her hand, and she blushed, batting her eyes at him from under thick, glossy fake eyelashes. Giant circles of rouge shone like identical orange suns on her weathered cheeks. When we walked away, he said, "Such a shame. Look what a drink can do." We greeted that lady in the same way for years thereafter, having the same conversation about her as we walked toward the cabanas, until one day Poppy told me she had died.

Nona and Poppy were at least three-times-a-week attendees of happy hours in North Miami Beach at any one of a rotation of six hotel or marina bars that served free food to catch the after-work crowd. They both collected Social Security and had drawers full of stolen pink Sweet'N Low packets and paper napkins. Poppy's work had been glamorous, but not as lucrative as it might have looked, and he had a gambling habit, spending long days at the horse and dog tracks. At happy hour, buying one drink entitled Nona and Poppy access to a decent appetizer buffet that served as their dinner. One of the buffets had barbecue ribs and sushi; another had tacos and quesadillas; a third featured a prime rib carving station.

One Friday we showed up at five p.m., few customers other than us in the hotel bar. Poppy, dressed all in white as usual, ushered us to a seat near the buffet.

"Please bring us two Bloody Marys," he told the waitress, indicating with a gesture that they were for himself and Nona, "With the vodka on the *side*. My little girl will have a soda."

The waitress appeared with two Bloody Marys, along with two elegant, stemmed shot glasses of vodka, and set them on the table.

"If you order tomato juice," Poppy said, pointing to the glasses, "it costs four dollars and seventy-five cents. If you order a Bloody Mary with vodka on the side at happy hour, it costs two dollars and seventy-five cents."

My soda was $3.50. I felt bad that I was too young to order the

Bloody Mary with the vodka on the side because it would have saved him seventy-five cents.

Poppy scanned the barroom and, when no one was looking, dumped the vodka shots into a plant behind him. That poor plant. I wondered if the vodka would kill it like it had killed the lady at the Surf Club.

ONCE, THE COUCH DRUNKS ARRIVED AS A COUPLE, A MAN AND HIS young wife. I overheard that they had moved into town and didn't have a place to stay. I didn't pay much attention to the history of our couch drunks and never asked questions. I didn't want to live symbiotically with them.

After a few nights and a few bottles of wine, the wife came into my room to play with my hamsters. She was pretty and a little chubby, with dark, platter-like eyes, and skin the color of doves. Her face brightened when she held the animals, baby-talking to them, asking me about their ages and what they liked to eat. She strolled the perimeter of my room, admiring my posters of horses, kittens, ducklings, and a shirtless John Stamos in tight leather pants.

"I'm wearing a wig," she said absently to a poster-size collage I had created from glossy pictures of horses cut from the pages of *Horse Fancy* magazine. The girl pulled on her dark, springy curls and turned to me. "This isn't my real hair."

She sat on the mattress on the floor in the corner of my room. The fact that I didn't have a *real* bed—one with a frame and a headboard—had traveled around school like a virus after a weekend sleepover, becoming taunting fodder for some of the mean girls, the same girls who called me "PYT" after the Michael Jackson song; instead of "pretty young thing," they cut the Y, shortened it to "PT," and changed the meaning to "prostitute." I hadn't even kissed a boy yet. My dad told me that a man's penis had sharp black barbs that shot from all sides of it, like a porcupine, and if I touched a penis I would experience the worst pain in the world and I'd have to go to the emergency room to have a hand operation to remove the black barbs and he'd *know* I had touched a penis and I'd be in *big* trouble. This information made going anywhere near boys kind of prohibitive. I didn't try to verify his claims, too embarrassed to ask anyone or open an anatomy book in the library.

"Really? That's not your hair?" I said to the couch drunk with the wig. "Can I see?"

She peeled back part of the wig near her forehead, revealing hair lighter than the dark wig's finger curls.

"It looks real," I said. "Why?"

"The man I'm with . . . he's not my husband," she said. "He kidnapped me from my mother. She used to beat me and she put her cigarette out on my neck." She swept back her wig hair to reveal a faint round scar in the hollow space between her clavicles. I couldn't imagine how a cigarette burn could be that unnoticeable, but I nodded in commiseration anyway.

"I'm thirteen," she said. "We . . . go to bed, you know, but we didn't for a long time. He didn't force me or anything."

My mouth must have been agape. I was also thirteen.

"He's going to buy me two kittens. I want the kittens with six toes," she said. She gazed at me with big, doleful eyes. "Nobody knows. Please don't tell anyone. He'll get mad."

"I won't," I told her. I felt violated, like it was me who had been kidnapped. Did her mother miss her? Was her family searching for her? How did she maneuver around the sharp black barbs shooting from the man's penis? I didn't want to ask.

I guessed I was the only other person in the world, besides her and her kidnapper/husband, who knew their secret, and I knew I should tell someone, but a secret was sacred, and at thirteen, that precept was gospel. I felt sorry for the girl, but also envious. I'd seen her drinking with my parents and her kidnapper/husband, and once I knew her secret, I resented being sent to bed while they continued their party. I was sure my parents didn't know about the couple's charade. Many years later, I finally broke her confidence, and my parents said they'd had no idea she was anything but a young adult.

I placed The Police's *Synchronicity* album onto my record player and set the needle to "Every Breath You Take." The girl and I sat together, silent, listening to Sting sing his haunting refrain: *I'll be watching you.*

Chapter 5

THE CREATURE WAS NOTHING BUT A PINK CURL, KNOBBY ON ITS sides, with silky, pearlescent yellow fluff rising from its back like vagrant weeds in an ill-tended garden. It slept hunched in the hollow of a few tissue papers. Its closed eyes were dark pebbles covered with the thinnest living tissue, arteries pulsing dangerously near the surface of its skin, red and blue highways on a trinket map. The hatchling looked barely contained within its membrane, as if the creature inside could spill out at will and rehatch itself into the world with one great push.

Then one eye squeezed open, glassy and black. The eye seemed knowing. I had thought of the little pink curl as an object; now it was looking at me. Its head popped up and it uttered a rodent-esque squeak, very un-bird-like, then scrunched its head into its neck and shimmied deeper into the tissue paper, falling back asleep.

Minutes before this creature found its way into my hands, I'd heard my boyfriend's Toyota engine whine and then stop with a putter. Out the window, I saw my boyfriend, Peter, walking up the blacktop holding a red-and-silver heart-shaped Mylar balloon that trailed behind him in the wind. I was eighteen years old, and I'd never before had a boyfriend on Valentine's Day. Peter, a student at Miami Dade Community College, where we both attended classes, had made dinner reservations for that night, but then called and asked to drop by a few hours earlier on his way home from work at the pet shop to give me something. In the hand not toting the end of the balloon's string, he held a white coffee mug encircled with a pattern of red hearts.

He thrust the mug at me in the open doorway.

"Happy Valentine's Day," he said and gave me a kiss. I reached for the mug with both hands, as if he were handing me the Holy Grail, and peered into it.

It definitely wasn't jewelry.

"It's a baby lovebird." Peter followed me inside. He let go of the balloon and it floated to the ceiling. "For Valentine's Day."

"I can see that." I cradled the mug in my hands. I hadn't anticipated this, though it wasn't beyond expectation that he'd give me a pet as a valentine.

I inspected the little parrot sleeping in the mug. I already had my share of pets: a ten-gallon tank of fish, each one named; a fat rabbit I'd found cold and starving under a bush near a soccer field; a dozen Mexican hooded rats; a gerbil; a Florida box tortoise named Swifty; a cage full of prolific zebra finches; and four cats, three of which I'd brought home as kittens—Paisley, the tiny feral gray tabby I picked out of a dumpster; Gladys, the chocolate Burmese someone gave to my dad; Emmeline, the fluffy black and white mute; and Sylvester, a smart tuxedo kitty whom I'd trained to give his paw to shake when asked.

The bird in the mug was plain and helpless, and I had the vague notion Peter had scored it for free. I stroked the creature with my index finger.

"I love it," I said, hoping he didn't hear the tentativeness in my voice.

Peter showed me how to heat the baby's premade hand-feeding formula in a small cup in the microwave, and how to fill a needleless syringe with the formula and place it on the baby's beak, which opened when touched. The bird's little head pumped up and down as I compressed the plunger of the syringe and its crop filled, the mustard-colored food visible in a pouch through the translucent skin under its neck. It looked like a bullfrog in mating season. I placed the baby back into the coffee mug, and it promptly fell asleep.

Peter drove away, leaving me alone with the little parrot and its Ziploc bag of supplies. What kind of person gives someone a Valentine's gift she has to feed every four hours? I stared at the delicate baby in my lap and thought about a name. Opal might be nice, but a resentful name choice, too, since opal was my birthstone and it was Valentine's Day, after all. I decided on Bonk, after a golden retriever in a movie I had recently seen. I sat on the sofa with Bonk's mug warming between my thighs and watched him sleep. He had tiny black spots all over his back where feathers threatened to burst through. His head was shaped like the round part of a question mark, and his body like a less-than symbol, angular and tapered to a point where his tail would be if feathers had been growing there. He squirmed, then delivered a forced-sounding noise like "eeeaahhhkkkk," followed by a loud, squirty poop.

I decided I could like the little guy.

BONK GREW AT A SUPERSONIC PACE, LIKE A STRANGE AMAZONIAN plant that sprouts a foot a day. He moved from the mug to a ten-gallon fish tank in a week. From one day to the next, the pepper-like black dots scattered on his skin burst through the thin tissue, forming pinfeathers that made him look like a pincushion with eyes. A few days later, an unnatural tropical green hue broke through the top of the pinfeathers. A shade of turquoise the ocean would envy covered his rump, and on his face, the slightest shade of pinkish peach emerged. His tail feathers unfurled from their sheathes in a combination of red, blue, black, and green. He loved when I scratched his head and face, helping him to preen away the waxy sheaths of the pinfeathers so the feathers could emerge.

His lust for food was ardent, and he'd eat from the syringe until he fell asleep on his feet. He'd nap in the front of my shirt after eating, wrapped in a paper towel to catch the inevitable poop.

"Look at that!" Poppy exclaimed when he met Bonk. "I am a great-grandfather! You are aging me, *Chérie.*"

Poppy held Bonk in one hand and petted him gently with the other, and I felt proud to have graduated to my own parrot.

"You are taking good care of him," Poppy said. "I would like to have a bird like this."

"Isn't he sweet?" I took Bonk from Poppy and cupped the baby in my hands.

"He is as sweet as his mother."

When Bonk saw me, he bounced around as if I was the sun and moon of his little birdy life. As soon as he gained some mobility, he paced frenetically back and forth in his fish tank when I walked into a room, cheeping like an alarm clock, and ceased only when he gained my attention. The more he needed me, the more I fell in love with him.

He'd cry and wail until I held his humid body in my hands; he'd ride on my shoulder while I did homework or chores. I'd watch television with him asleep under my chin, and I wouldn't move if it meant I might wake him. I saw countless episodes of *Alf* and *The Golden Girls* I had not intended to watch.

How could this animal be capable of such trust? I'd known birds as cautious creatures. Bonk preened me and cuddled me and argued with me when I did something he didn't like, such as blow my nose. Tissues were offensive and had to be shredded, which he did while screaming with the verve of pumped-up troops running into battle.

The African peach-faced lovebird, Bonk's species, is a member of the *Agapornis* genus, whose name stems from the Greek word *agape*, meaning "love." *Ornis* means "bird." The field scientist who named these little parrots couldn't have been more accurate. Bonk exuded love from every cell of his birdy body.

At three months old, he was feathered and mobile, running after me wherever I went. He was supposed to be off the hand-feeding formula by then, but I'd never hand-fed a baby bird before, and I indulged his relentless begging. He squalled and bobbed up and down like an oil derrick on speed, and I couldn't do anything until I fed him. He ate formula for six months, way longer than he should have, and became big and bright and attached to me like a rivet, an obsessive kind of friendship that wasn't one-sided.

MY PARENTS AND I MOVED TO A SUNNY HOUSE ON THE WATER IN A section of Miami called King's Bay, south of Kendall and north of Homestead, an outcropping of postwar houses on streets lined with old shade trees. My dad wanted a home with a dock and easy access to good fishing spots in the bay. The back of our house opened onto a wide canal leading to the sea on one end and, on the other, to a boat basin where homes had large yachts tied to their docks. It was the perfect house for Bonk. I could sit outside with him in the sun and ocean breeze, or under the sea grape tree for shade, and he had his own little room off the kitchen, the "bird room," where he could hop around without concern of becoming lost or injured.

I referred to Bonk as "my little son." He spent most of his days on my shoulder, perched under my hair, sleeping or quibbling with the tag on the back of my shirt. He attended college classes with me at Miami Dade, enjoyed keg parties with Peter and his frat guy friends, shopped at the mall, went to the monthly meeting of the Florida chapter of the Cockatiel and African Lovebird Society, and tagged along on my dates with Peter, unnoticed underneath my long hair until he decided to chirrup. He learned to click and whistle, and greeted me every day with a resounding catcall.

I took Bonk with me whenever I spent the night with Nona and Poppy. The sun clocked out as Nona cooked fish stew and okra in tomato sauce, and served us hummus and olives, and pita bread straight from her oven. Poppy and I rested in squeaky patio chairs, feet up on a plastic patio table, watching his Lady Gouldian and zebra finches—and Bonk, the little bird excited by dusk after a day of napping in the heat. Poppy loved when Bonk drank water: the way the bird dipped his beak into the bowl, then tilted his head back so the water rolled down his throat. Poppy pointed to Bonk as he drank so I wouldn't miss it, and peeled cucumbers and boiled eggs for Bonk so he had something soft and nutritious to eat.

Bonk ate at the dinner table with me every night and shared my food in the cafeteria on campus, jumping into the meal, his reptilian feet leaving gravy tracks on the table. He had issues with silverware, and ran between place settings to toss the spoons, forks, and knives onto the floor. It was difficult to keep him out of drinking glasses. He'd bathe standing on the edge of the glass, spraying water like a dog shaking off a swim. I had to give him a shallow water glass of his own or he'd bathe in my orange soda.

"Please do not kiss the bird on the mouth, *Chérie*," Poppy said, catching me allowing Bonk to clean my teeth one day, his feet perched on my bottom lip and the front half of his body all the way inside my mouth, picking at my molars. Bonk was a good and gentle dentist.

"Go brush your teeth," Poppy ordered, pointing to the bathroom. I had a penchant for kissing Bonk on the beak; he could bite through my lip if he wanted to, but he was delicate as a flower floating on the surface of a pond.

"When I was in Egypt, I had three beautiful cousins die of parrot fever."

Poppy had told me the story a hundred times. I was sympathetic, but I didn't want any obstructions in my relationship with Bonk. Psittacosis—parrot fever—killed many people in Egypt in the 1930s, according to Poppy, but I knew Bonk didn't have it. I plunked my little son onto my shoulder, locked myself in the bathroom, and ran the water to humor Poppy, but didn't brush my teeth.

Peter's Valentine's Day gift started to become more important to me than Peter, which was significant, since I had suffered a crush on Peter since eleventh grade. Most days after school that year, I drove to Super Pet Mart, where he was the assistant manager, and I'd linger in the aisles to watch the red factor canaries sing, the ferrets and hedgehogs sleep, and the kittens play, not because I wanted these animals, but because I desired Peter's attention. I'd stand near the rodent section and ask him about the Russian hamsters, the long-haired mice, and the baby guinea pigs.

I lurked among the dark rows of fish tanks stacked four high, the chaotic underwater world darting around in bright flashes. I'd ask him about puffer fish, anemones, and water turtles—so many questions that he'd become irritated and pawn me off onto another employee. Peter was several years older than I was, cute and husky, and he limped a little from a high school baseball knee injury, but he knew a lot about animals, and I found that sexy. It seemed to me we were kindred spirits, even if he didn't know it.

After graduating from Miami Palmetto Senior High, I enrolled at Miami Dade Community College, where Peter was a part-time student. During my first semester, I followed him to a frat party and talked with him into the night, winning his heart with my knowledge of birds and Bob Marley.

The summer before I turned nineteen, he hired me at the pet store as the "fish girl." I took care of dozens of fish tanks, a job I adored, since I could bring Bonk to work. I learned how to clean gravel and slope it toward the back of the tanks so they looked bigger. I changed water and measured salinity. I learned the names and particulars of hundreds of fish species, and discovered which fish lived together peaceably and which would eat one another. Sometimes Bonk ran down my arm to quibble with the fish, and I had to pluck him up before he jumped in with the neon tetras.

Bonk shunned almost everyone, and when he felt threatened by someone standing nearby, he'd run down my arm, beak open, tongue waggling, and lunge at the marauder. At five inches tall, he was an alligator wrestler in a little bird's body. I felt safe with Bonk, my mini green guard dog.

"Get that brat away from me," Peter warned as Bonk planted a well-placed bite on his arm, hand, or neck, picking the bird up in his fist and handing him to me the way someone would hang up a phone. I'd apologize and try to maintain a neutral expression, but I wasn't sorry. No one came between Bonk and me, not even the person who brought us together.

When I had to lock Bonk in his cage, he complained and performed a frantic door dance, running back and forth in front of the cage door, rattling it like a thirsty prisoner, yawping as if tortured. He learned how to open the doors to his cage, and I had to clip them shut. He was a bird genius, coming when I called him, like a maniacal green Chihuahua running across the carpet, up the fabric of my clothing and onto my shoulder. I kept his wings clipped so he wouldn't fly away when I took him outside. It upset me to clip him, but I didn't want to lose him to an appealing updraft or olive tree.

Bonk's intense likes and dislikes surprised me. He despised not only tissues, but full cups of food—he'd burrow into a cup of seed, scattering it three feet around his cage, then stand by the empty dish, sticking his head in and out as if he wondered where the seed went. He was strange around money: he'd argue with a penny, screaming at it and flipping it over until it fell off the surface of the table or he'd shoved it under something.

"You are starting to look alike," Poppy teased, when I showed up with Bonk on my shoulder. Bonk had his own cage at Nona and Poppy's place.

"That's OK," I said. "Bonk is much prettier than me."

"Heavens forbid," Poppy said, holding his palms up to the ceiling.

"You think I'm prettier than a bird?"

"You are prettier than all the birds in the world."

"I don't think so." I handed Bonk to Poppy, and the bird bit him hard on the webbing between thumb and forefinger. Poppy shook his hand and Bonk fell to the floor. Bonk stretched himself up on tippy toes, flapped his wings, and chirruped loudly.

"This bird loves you," Poppy said, inspecting his hand. "And only you."

Bonk loved small, dark places, too, such as the insides of shoes and the space under my bed covers. He was a little messy, but since he was such a small bird, his messes were small, too. Once, someone at a gas station asked me if I had a bird and I said yes, proudly, thinking he had seen me somewhere with Bonk until he pointed out a squiggle of dried bird poop on my T-shirt.

Our four cats—Emmeline, Paisley, Gladys, and Sylvester—didn't take an interest in Bonk. Paisley, the gray tabby feral I'd fished from a dumpster when she was a tiny kitten with her eyes still closed, caught wild birds a few times and brought them into the house—doves mostly, to my horror. I put bells on the cats to prevent a backyard bird slaughter, and kept a close watch on the cats when Bonk was out of his cage—there were plenty of birds outside for them to stalk, and indoors it was easier to sprawl in a beam of sunshine on the slate floor and groom one another's ears.

Bonk had a fondness for chewing the plastic off the ends of shoelaces, so it was difficult to relace my shoes should the lace slip out. He stole and chewed my pen caps into anthills of plastic. All my pens dried out and I had to throw them away. Each morning, while I put on makeup, Bonk fought ferociously with his reflection in the bathroom mirror.

When we settled down to watch television or read a book, he'd sit on my forehead, grip my bangs, and preen my eyebrows, one hair at a time. He'd peer inside my ears and trim my nail cuticles. He spent hours "picking off" the freckles on my arms and neck, and I let him do it because it was a good service, if a futile one, though he could pinch like a wire cutter with his sharp beak.

After a year, Peter fired me from the pet store, blaming it on the manager, mumbling something about cutbacks. He didn't want me around anymore. He worked six days a week and liked to carouse with his pals on the weekends. I was underage and couldn't go to bars. Then I heard he'd bought a lovebird for another girl.

He came over during one of our big fights to take back his scuba equipment, which he kept in our garage because he liked to practice diving in the waterway behind our house. Before he arrived I put on every bit of his scuba equipment, from the wet suit to the flippers, hauled the heavy tanks onto my back, put the mask on my face, stuck the buoyancy compensator valve in my mouth, and did a penguin dance in front of the picture window as he thumped on the door, shaking my butt and wiggling my hips, flapping my feet around in a circle, flashing him my best jazz hands. I thought he'd laugh.

He kicked the door and his foot walloped through it, wood

cracking and a panel of the door splintering at my feet. I flip-flapped in the black flippers like a terrified penguin toward the phone to call 911, but he reached through the hole in the door, unlocked it, rushed inside, and grabbed the phone from my hand, pulling the cord from the wall. I closed my eyes, waiting for a blow to the face or something equally furious; instead, he cried. He begged me to tell my parents that the cats whacked the foot-size hole in the door, but that was ridiculous. My parents demanded I never see him again. Poppy said if Peter wanted to speak with me, he would have to knock on the door with his foot—gently—because his arms would be so full of presents and flowers. Short of that, which wasn't going to happen, Peter was persona non grata.

I didn't want anything around that reminded me of Peter. I tossed or regifted everything he had ever given me, but I convinced myself that Bonk wasn't in any way associated with him. Bonk was a bird of my making, a creation of my love and attention, rarer than opals.

Chapter 6

"MORNING, BONK!" I SANG, WALKING DOWN THE HALL AFTER I woke, whistling a catcall. That whistle was our "contact call," a specific sound many species of birds repeat between partners or offspring to communicate location and well-being when the partner is out of sight. I was an honorary bird.

Bonk was almost two years old and I was nearly twenty, and we'd done this ritual since Bonk could catcall. After washing my face and brushing my teeth, I beelined for his cage to say good morning and feed and water him, whistling as I approached. This morning, Bonk didn't catcall back.

I found him crouched at the bottom of his cage, feathers fluffed and ruffled, hunched in a back corner. He didn't dance or beg to sit on my shoulder, wail to be let out, or rattle the cage door. I opened the cage and he hissed at me. He gaped his beak wide, black tongue waggling, and snapped at my hand.

I tried to coax him from the corner with a pen cap, but he hissed in short bursts, and fluffed his neck feathers, like a dog raises its hackles. I filled his food dish and that brought him out of the corner. There was a white oblong object at the bottom of the cage. Bonk ate a few seeds, then rushed back to the object and settled himself—no, *herself*—back onto it.

Bonk was a hen. Push me over with a feather.

Parrots, like chickens, can lay infertile eggs. Although no chick will ever hatch from an infertile egg, the bird is nonetheless protective of it. Bonk defended and warmed that infertile egg. Her life became centered on it, and she didn't want anything to do with me anymore.

How could she forget the relationship we had forged over the past two years, all those days of hand-feeding, the ruined shoe-laces, our sitcom nights? Perhaps in the same way a doting mother doesn't want to lose a child to teenage-hood, I didn't want to lose my Bonk to an *egg*.

I had no idea what to do. Should I take her egg away? I considered that cruel, and she wouldn't let me near it anyway. On Tuesday, four days after Bonk laid her egg, I attended the monthly meeting of the Florida chapter of the Cockatiel and African Love-bird Society. We met inside a junior high school at eight in the evening and listened to lectures by local veterinarians, bird breeders, and genetics experts. Sometimes members prepared lectures on proper feeding, cage building, or hurricane preparation. Between twenty and thirty people showed up, all much older than myself, mostly retirees. I couldn't wait to tell them about the egg.

"Where's your little peachie?" asked Marge, the club's treasurer, a retired grandmother who bred lovebirds and cockatiels.

"Bonk had an *egg*," I said, forming an egg shape with my fingers to show her how big it was.

"That's wonderful!" she said. "Now you can breed her. It's great to have a healthy egg-laying hen."

"But she doesn't like me anymore."

"She'll like you again as soon as you take away the egg."

"She won't let me near it."

"Let her sit on it for a week, then put on some gloves and take it away. In no time she'll be your buddy again. It's the same when they have babies."

"Isn't that . . . *mean?*" I said.

"It's meaner to let her sit for weeks on an egg that won't hatch," Marge said. "It's a waste of her time and takes away from her happiness. She'll never have a baby from an infertile egg, and that's got to be more frustrating than anything."

Other group members suggested removing all paper material from Bonk, even the newspaper lining her cage. Shredding paper stimulates breeding behavior in lovebird hens. Bonk shredded any bit of paper in her reach—newspaper, paperback books, tissue boxes—into thin, identical strips, and stuffed them between the turquoise feathers of her rump. This is how peach-faced lovebirds transport nesting material. Male lovebirds don't do this, so it's a reliable way to tell the difference between genders. I must have been daydreaming in some of the bird society meetings, because I hadn't registered that before.

Poppy arranged to pick me up to spend the night with him and Nona that weekend, saying he had errands nearby. I don't think he had errands—he didn't want to worry about me on the road by myself. I was excited to show him the egg.

"She will not have a baby from that egg," he said, bending at cage level to peer at Bonk as I lured her out of the corner with a wooden spatula.

"I know."

"She might have more eggs."

"I know."

"She wants a boyfriend."

"I know."

"What do you *not* know, *Chérie?*"

"I don't know how to take it away from her."

"Do you want my help?"

"I'm not ready," I said.

He put his arm around my shoulder and we watched Bonk for a minute as she warmed her egg, eyeing us like a security guard.

"You are a good mother."

We left, and it was the first time since I'd had Bonk that she didn't accompany me for a sleepover at Nona and Poppy's apartment. I was lonely without her.

I let the cranky, protective new "mom" pamper her single egg for well over a week. Then, with an acidic taste in my mouth and trembling hands, I slid on my mother's yellow dishwashing gloves.

I tiptoed to the cage and stood for a long time, watching Bonk. She huddled in the corner, crouched on top of her egg, watching me. It was a face-off, nose to beak.

Bonk rushed at me with her beak wide as I pulled the cage door open. I distracted her using a pencil and led her away from the egg. She bit the pencil eraser off and fought with the crimped silver ferrule. With my other gloved hand, I reached toward the egg and removed it from the cage.

Bonk hurried to the corner where her egg had been. She seemed disoriented for a minute, then hopped to her food dish and began munching the end off a carrot.

In the kitchen, I rested the warm egg on a bed of cotton balls in a plastic container and studied it. It looked like a miniature chicken egg, the same color and shape. Bonk's egg ranked among my prize possessions. I found clear nail polish in my mother's bathroom cabinet and sat at the kitchen counter and painted the egg so it would last. I placed her egg and its cotton-wad nest on a bookshelf in my room, high enough so Bonk wouldn't see it.

Bonk and I renewed our friendship, but I couldn't stop obsessing about the egg. Maybe Bonk needed a mate. I didn't want to breed her, but I did want her to have a companion, so I bought a black-masked lovebird.

Breeding the black-masked with the peach-faced lovebird

would create a hybrid bird, often called a "mule" because they're infertile, a taboo in the bird community. I didn't intend on breeding the two birds, so I didn't give them a nest or any paper to shred. I named the new bird Baby. He had a striking black head, a body covered in blue hues ranging from sky to sapphire to royal, and a thick white collar around his neck like a nobleman in a Renaissance painting.

Baby was skittish and scrambled to the back of the cage when I put my hand inside to retrieve him, though once free from the cage he was happy to settle on my shoulder or fall asleep under my chin. When Bonk met Baby she ran at him, beak open, and dove for his toes to chomp them off. After a month there was no change in the behavior of either bird, so I bought a Fischer's lovebird and named him Smidge, a feisty red-beaked youngster who bit hard when he didn't get his way. He liked to bite my neck, and he didn't like Bonk or Baby at all. The three birds lived in the same room in separate cages for several months, with no interaction between any of them. Bonk laid more eggs.

So did Baby and Smidge.

I had three hens.

After another trip to a bird breeder's house with my parents, who had offered to buy me a few lovebirds, and two *more* females—now I had five lovebirds—I discovered how to make an educated guess about lovebird gender. Peach-faced and masked lovebirds are monomorphic, meaning that there are no real visible differences between the genders, but a knowledgeable lovebird keeper notices the subtle variances.

Female lovebirds are often larger than males, and have a feistier personality; the male's bone structure is finer and his personality is easygoing and gentle if he's tame. A female's hip bones, which can be felt by placing a finger on her vent (also called the cloaca, where feces is expelled), are wider and the bones are blunter than the male's, whose hip bones are often sharp and closer together.

I called Marge from the lovebird club and told her I wanted to find a mate for Bonk and not keep guessing about gender. I also told her I wanted a lutino male—bright yellow body with a red face—so the babies would hatch out pied. Pied was my favorite color mutation at the time, a lovebird with feathers of varying colors smattered onto one individual like a Jackson Pollock painting.

"That's not how it works, girl," she said. "You can't put a green bird and a yellow bird together and come out with pied babies."

"Green plus yellow doesn't equal pied?"

"There has to be pied in the bird's genetics. One of the parents has to be either pied or split to pied."

I focused on finding a male, no matter the color mutation. Within a month, Bonk had accepted Binky, a year-old male peach-faced lovebird that looked like her.

I hung a wooden nest box in their cage, and a few weeks later Bonk laid five eggs. Each of those eggs was a revelation. I wanted to hold them, to witness the movements inside each moony shell. I spent a lot of time sitting by the cage, watching Bonk and Binky hop in and out of the wooden nest box, Binky feeding Bonk by regurgitating his food into her beak at the entrance to the nest as she warmed the eggs. Female lovebirds brood their eggs, unlike cockatiels and pigeons, who share egg-warming duties, though at night both lovebird parents will sleep inside the nest.

After a few weeks, peeping erupted from the nest, cheeping impossibly loud for a baby bird, amplified by the acoustics inside the wooden box. I shined a flashlight into the entry hole. Bonk backed into a corner, hissing, beak open, tongue wagging. I taunted her out of her box with a pen near the nest's hole, and when she hopped out to attack I saw a little pink coil wriggling on its back next to four eggs, a loud, wailing baby like Bonk had been, but pinker and wrigglier.

I called Poppy.

"Now I am a great-*great* grandfather, *Chérie!*" he said. "What are you doing to me? People will believe me to be much older than I am."

Two more of Bonk's eggs hatched in the next few days. Watching the three babies grow was phenomenal, like watching a storm roll over the ocean. Every moment brought something new, a shift in color or pattern. They sat together in a green lump and scrambled away from me when I opened the box. I wanted to hold them, but Bonk wouldn't let me.

Bonk and Binky proved to be devoted parents. Binky fed Bonk, who returned inside to feed the chicks. About nine weeks after they hatched, the babies fledged, venturing from the box for short periods, and rushing back inside when I entered the room. A few weeks after that, Bonk wouldn't let them back into the nest, nipping them if they tried to squeeze through the round opening. She had laid another egg.

In the short time between Bonk finding her mate and her babies fledging from the nest, I collected more than thirty new lovebirds. I put them to nest, and hand-fed the two-week-old chicks so my babies would be tame. I built rough-looking flight cages and aviaries to house the babies. The world dissolved when I tended to the birds, and I wanted more of that feeling. I needed more birds.

Chapter 7

UNTIL THE AGE OF TWELVE I HAD HAD BOTH FEET IN POPPY'S TEETO-taler camp, save the odd sips of wine or beer from an adult's glass, to taste. Sliding into thirteen, I'd had my doubts. What was the big deal? Drinking looked fun and grown-up, and I wanted nothing more than to be an adult. If I drank alcohol I'd grow up faster.

Some of the kids I knew had bars in their houses, or collections of liquor bottles in kitchen cabinets. Sometimes we'd sip the peppermint or peach schnapps, then pour water into the bottle to make up the deficit. I liked the sting and heat, and the way a small taste pirouetted to my head.

One mom I knew was drunk all the time. She was the wife of a drug dealer who bought Ferraris from my dad, so it was easy to steal booze from the wet bar by the pool when my dad took me there to spend the night with the drug dealer's three redheaded daughters. Once, their mom, all cheetah print pants and off-the-shoulder T-shirt, staggered into the bedroom where we were sprawled in front of the television, and slurred, "Are you girls listening to Jeff Leper?" We had Duran Duran's "Girls on Film" video playing on MTV, but we knew she meant Def Leppard and we laughed. I liked taking sips of alcohol, but I never wanted to get *that* kind of drunk.

My parents didn't toss vodka into plants like Poppy did. They didn't drink vodka. They drank beer and wine. Beer was disgusting, and I couldn't drink half a bottle of wine, pour water into it, and expect to escape notice. There was no way to sneak alcohol at home, but my parents had a "European" idea about the relationship between children and alcohol: they thought if they made it off-limits when I was young, I'd want it more when I grew up. Working on this theory, I asked for wine every time they drank it. At a restaurant, they'd pour a tiny pool of red wine into a wineglass and fill the rest of the glass with water. My dad had been given wine at lunch in grammar school in Paris, and he didn't understand the strange taboo Americans had about alcohol.

I'd study their wineglasses as they sipped, making the wine last through dinner. I gulped my glassful. The wine alchemized the water into a coarse, curly feeling juice that puckered my tongue. I'd ask for another. I could manage ten glasses before my mom cut me off, then I'd spend the next hour melting cocktail straws into the candle on the table, fascinated at how they disappeared as the flame licked the red plastic.

Just before Christmas, the year I turned thirteen, I asked Poppy to sew me a raw silk black-and-white pinstriped pleated skirt for a holiday party my parents and I attended every year at their friends' home in Coral Gables. Poppy sewed beautiful one-of-a-kind clothes for me whenever I needed something to wear for a party or the science fair at school. I had seen the black-and-white silk in his studio and loved the way it felt, soft and nubby, with enough starchiness to keep the pleats neat. My mom liked to dress me like a little girl, in baby doll dresses; that year, even though I didn't own a bra yet, I wanted something grown-up.

I paired the new pinstriped skirt—which I loved—with a red sweater, white tights, and black patent leather Mary Janes. I wasn't allowed to wear makeup, but I did have lip gloss, so I shined my lips and scrunched my hair into ringlets, appearing like a child in the mirror. I had been aiming at teenager.

The party was held at a large home with a hacienda feel, sliding glass doors and plate glass windows overlooking a central courtyard with a stone fountain. Terra-cotta flagstones led us from the driveway to the courtyard into the Christmas party, me hopping from stone to stone as if they were a hopscotch grid. My shiny Mary Janes reflected the blinking holiday lights, and I felt fancy in the silk skirt. Other guests wore slinky gold camisoles and tailored blazers, their jewelry glinting like sunlight on water. It was a party out of a TV commercial, revelers' heads tossed back, mouths open in laughter, almost in slow motion.

A waiter with a tray of champagne glasses greeted us. The blonde liquid imitated the lights from the Christmas tree and sparkled red, green, and gold, blinking and bubbling. I gazed at the array of glasses, and one of my earliest memories projected onto the tray—me at five years old, holding my mom's hand at the Museum of Modern Art in New York City, van Gogh's *Starry Night* hanging far above my head, feeling transported by the yellow swirls against a sea of raven blue, not having words for the vision, only awe.

I reached for a glass of champagne.

"What are you doing?" My mom tried to seize the glass, so I gripped it harder.

My dad waved a hand in the air, as if to clear away smoke. "Let her have it," he said. "It's fine. It's Christmas."

My mom looked at me as if to say, "You got away with it this time," then released my glass.

The champagne lit my throat and chest. I liked the way the

bubbles felt on my lips and the way the glass looked in my hand, like a crystal flower. I felt imbued with grown-up-ishness.

I assessed the situation. If I walked around the party, away from my parents, and gulped this glass of champagne, I could grab another from a cruising waiter and make it seem like the same glass. My parents were preoccupied at parties; this was going to be easy. I slipped away from my mom, drank my first glass and pinched another from a tray, toured the courtyard, and did it again. Then again. I met my mom at the buffet table and piled a red plastic plate full of spiral-cut ham and baby quiches.

"Is that the same glass?" my mom asked. She squinted her eyes at me. She knew it wasn't.

I reeled to the bar, tended by my childhood acquaintances, two boys three years older than I was, kids of my parents' friends. On earlier occasions, they had delighted in covering themselves in ketchup and chasing me all over their houses, screaming that they had been stabbed and that the ketchup was blood. They'd terrified me. Now, behind the bar, they seemed like adults, though they couldn't have been more than sixteen. They asked what I was drinking and I told them.

"Here, try this," one of them said, handing me a squat glass filled with ice and dark soda.

"What is it?" I said, smelling the drink.

"Rum and Coke."

The drink was sweet, but I winced from the rum. It tasted like lightning.

I sprawled on a bed in a dark room, pink satin comforter and pink and white pillows beneath my head. My shoes were off. A dim light in the room radiated from the open bathroom door. The ceiling spun. No, the bed spun. No, the entire room spun, in tight circles. The bed lifted off the floor and revolved when I closed my eyes. I opened my eyes and the bed landed with a clunk. I moaned and called out for my mom, but the walls swallowed my voice.

Then came the projectile vomit onto the bed with the pink satin comforter, onto the pink plush carpeting, and all over the pink striped wallpaper. I sat up with vomit on my hands and face. Another wave of sickness. I fell off the bed and crawled to the bathroom, vomiting honey baked ham and quiche on the way, and vomited on the white tiled bathroom floor before making it to the toilet. I rested my head on the cool seat and vomited into the toilet and all over it.

Someone woke me up after I don't know how long. I had fallen asleep—or passed out—on the bathroom floor. The outline of the lady who owned the house appeared, a blurred vision dazzled by the mirror's vanity lights. My mom stood behind her.

Then it was morning. I didn't remember how I arrived home or how I had gotten into an oversized white T-shirt. The ends of my hair were crusty. My beautiful pinstriped skirt hung over my desk chair, rumpled and covered in vomit. The corner of the room spun a little and my tongue felt hairy.

"Hey, Miss Champagne," my dad said as I shuffled into the living room. He sat on the couch smoking a cigarette, leafing through *The Boat Trader*. "How many glasses did you have last night?"

"I don't know," I croaked, holding my forehead, afraid to look at him.

"You threw up all over their room."

"I know," I said, waiting for my punishment. Maybe I'd have to go back and clean it up.

"That'll teach you. You can't handle your liquor." He patted the couch and I plopped down beside him. "What did you drink?"

"I had champagne and then the boys gave me a rum and Coke."

"There you go," he said. "Never, *ever*, mix alcohols. That's what got you sick."

We weren't invited to that party again.

But it was not *my* last party. I attended George Washington Carver Junior High for seventh grade, then Ponce de Leon for eighth, and finally Miami Palmetto for ninth, and I drank as much as I could in those years, sneaking sips from other kids' parents' stocked bars. During my three years at Miami Palmetto Senior High School, my friends and I bribed people outside of convenience stores to buy us Boone's Farm Strawberry Hill wine and Bartles & Jaymes wine coolers. We drank in cars, at movies, at the planetarium during Pink Floyd laser light shows, and even at lunchtime during school. High school went by in a blur of Thunderbird and Mad Dog 20/20. Despite all the vomiting and violated curfews, I did manage to graduate.

I DRANK ON WEEKENDS IN COLLEGE, PRIME DRINKING YEARS FOR most students, but because I had the birds I didn't need the distraction of great quantities of alcohol, and I couldn't take good care of my baby birds if I was drunk. As my bird breeding hobby grew, drinking became less of an activity for me. I didn't have many friends to drink with anyway. The birds weren't ersatz friends—they were true compatriots.

My parents indulged my bird hobby. When I brought a bird home—or another fish tank, turtle, or rodent—either my parents wouldn't notice or they'd show interest in the new creatures. If I brought a dog into the house—which I did many times, scooping strays off the street—they wouldn't let the mutt past the threshold. We'd had Dobermans and a Pomeranian when I was younger, but my folks were done with dogs. If I tried bringing another kitten home—we had four cats already—their fingers pointed to the door before I could say, "Can we keep him?" My parents both loved animals, and my dad was particularly emotionally invested in our cat, Gladys, calling her name every day the *second* he stepped into the front door after work, waiting for her to curl around his legs and say hello in her emphatic Burmese yowl. So I couldn't understand why *more* didn't equal *better*. I'd call Poppy in tears, begging him to reason with my parents about a new kitten or stray dog, but he'd defer to them and instruct me to respect my parents' wishes.

Chapter 8

AFTER GRADUATING FROM COMMUNITY COLLEGE WITH AN ASSOCI-
ate's degree in liberal arts, I began studies at Florida International
University, and sat in the front row of my literature class. The
professor stood near the blackboard discussing *The Handmaid's
Tale* by Margaret Atwood, a dystopian novel about the oppression
of women, when my clutch of lovebird babies cheeped simultane-
ously inside the plastic critter keeper under my desk. There was
no mistaking the ratcheting cry of baby birds. I tapped the container with my fingernail and the cheeping ceased. My professor
stopped talking, scanned the room, and resumed lecturing.

In unison, the baby birds tattled on me again. I tapped their
container and they quieted. The professor glared at me.

"What's going on?" she said, the open novel limp in her hand.

"Sorry, I have baby birds," I said. I was a little embarrassed,
but mostly anxious. My babies were hungry.

She squinted at me. "You're the strangest student I've ever
had," she said, before turning back to the chalkboard.

After class, I crossed the grassy quad to the cafeteria. I filled a
cup with hot water meant for tea and carried it, along with my

babies and my backpack, to a table far from the cashiers. I stirred the mustard-colored powdered hand-feeding formula into the hot water until it reached a gruel-like consistency, then added a spoonful of banana and yams baby food to the concoction, and half a teaspoon of peanut butter. I tested the formula against my upper lip to gauge the temperature.

My six lovebird babies stretched their necks and cheeped like scratchy records when I opened the critter keeper. They were three and four weeks old, covered in downy fluff, their black eyes open, specks of contour feathers threatening to burst from their skin. Each had the beginnings of wings and a tail, the vivid blues, greens, and yellows startling against their baby fluff.

Lovebird babies always feather out the same way: first the wings, head, and tail, and last the body. As the feathers grow, the little downy puff of feather fluff preceding the feather stays glued on at the tip, a remnant of the juvenile downy coat that kept the baby warm before its feathers emerged. This piece of fluff eventually falls off, or I'd pick it off. If the baby was a green mutation the fluff was pinkish at first, and if it was a blue mutation, the fluff was white. Juvenile lovebirds also have a dark top mandible (the top of the beak) that lightens as the bird matures, which is a good way to tell the adults from the juveniles.

I placed several napkins onto the table and removed the babies from the plastic container, then filled a needle-less syringe with formula and placed it inside each baby's beak. The babies pumped their little heads up and down, swallowing the formula until their crops filled like balloons. Most birds have a crop, a stretchy, saclike organ below the esophagus. Below that is the proventriculus, which secretes enzymes to help digest the food, which then travels to the gizzard, a muscular stomach that grinds the hard food birds typically eat. I stopped feeding before their crops became too full—the crop can become stretched, and bacteria may grow in the crevices.

Once the babies ate, they clumped themselves inside the critter keeper and fell asleep on top of one another in a pile of skin and feet. I arrived late for my philosophy class, but at least my babies wouldn't interrupt our discussion of Aristotle.

Maybe I *was* a weird student. Bonk had become the be-all and end-all of birdness for me, and I had embarked on a search for that kind of love in everything feathered from then on, mostly in the form of lovebirds, the purest form of love and grace I had ever known. Someone left a well-behaved red-lored Amazon parrot named Miami Bird with me for boarding and never picked her up, so I added her to my flock. She taught a lot of the lovebirds to catcall, and I spent hours training her to do a variety of tricks, from spinning on her perch to waving hello.

Naughty little Bonk liked to stand on the books I was studying and shred the tops of each page, so I couldn't sell back my college textbooks. When I typed my term papers she hopped onto the keyboard and picked at the keys until I plucked her back onto my shoulder. She stole the question mark key and I had to glue it back in place.

I SPENT WEEKENDS TRAVELING TO BIRD CLUB MEETINGS AND BIRD shows and expos all over Florida, showing my birds in competitions and winning ribbons and trophies. Sometimes Poppy came with me. The birds took up a generous part of my everyday life. My flock needed to be fed and cleaned every morning, which took well over an hour, and then tended for an hour in the evening. The lovebird babies needed feeding and cleaning at least four times a day. I did my chores by rote, considering them more a blessing than a burden. When Bonk wasn't nesting, she'd ride on my shoulder and chirp into my ear as I cleaned cages and fed her flock mates. There were avian details to memorize and consummate, too—how to pull a blood feather from a bird's wing in case of emergency; how to hold a bird around the neck rather than its body because birds breathe differently than humans; how to recognize the signs of avian illness; how to stop bleeding; and how to know if a change in attitude was hormonal, behavioral, or medical.

I spent hours memorizing the Latin names for the bird species I wanted, peeling through the pages of Joseph Forshaw's *Parrots of the World*, a huge illustrated book with images of every parrot in the known universe. The lovebird species sounded like poetry: *Agapornis roseicollis, Agapornis fischeri, Agapornis personata*. I'd lie in bed staring into the darkness and repeat those names over and over until sleep came. They felt like a safety blanket. My peers in college participated in activities that created opportunities to socialize with associates and colleagues later in life—tennis, skiing, sailing, chess. I played with birds.

"YOU NEED TO FIND A MAN," DR. ZIELEZIENSKI, MY AVIAN VETERI-narian, admonished every time I saw her, which was often as my flock grew. I knew I'd found a compatriot in birds when I met Dr. Z, an avian wizard, able to handle the most bronco of parrots. She had a wry sense of humor, the slightest Virginia twang, and a sweet, reassuring, respectful manner, even when she chastised me for being bird addicted.

"You're spending too much time with these birds," she'd say as I waltzed into the office with a bird carrier in hand, a new bundle of feathers inside. "Do you have a life at all? Are you dating?"

Dr. Z had been recently married, and was newly evangelistic about the value of a social life. I'd assure her I was dating, but, in truth, I spent much of my time scribbling formulas for lovebird genetics using Punnett squares and obsessing about creating a variety of rare lovebird colors in my flock. Poppy encouraged me not to date—no surprise there after the Peter fiasco—saying I was too young to be attached to one man. Heeding that advice, I saved most of my energy for the birds.

If I could sleuth out the background colors, patterns, and dominant and recessive traits for lovebirds in my breeding program, I could predict what color babies they'd have, and manipulate those genes to attain colors I wanted to produce. From the obvious genetics of my parent birds—what they looked like on the outside, their dominant genes—I could predict some color mutations in my babies. But I didn't know the background of most of my birds, so I had to guess about the parents' genetics based on the colors they threw in each clutch of chicks. Lovebird genetics are complex, because they're not all about dominant and recessive genes; there are incomplete-dominant traits, sex-linked traits, and dark factors.

New colors and patterns—called mutations—appear every year, and become the color du jour that breeders want in their flocks. Birds with new colors cost upward of four to six hundred dollars—funds I didn't have. I produced genetic maps to create new mutations within my own flock. It could take me five generations to develop a color I wanted.

As my baby birds matured, I gave Poppy his choice of them, so his flock became nearly as large as mine, and he started breeding lovebirds, too. His birds—my babies—seemed healthier than my birds, bigger and shinier, happier. I didn't know what we were doing differently. He had a synchronous relationship with the birds that I didn't have yet.

Bonk and I spent long, lazy days with Poppy on his screened balcony watching his lovebirds eat, drink, and tend to their young in the salt air after he and Nona sold the house with the coop and moved to a fourth-floor condo in Sunny Isles, Miami Beach, our pigeons having long ago flown away. Nona would call us inside for a Greek feast: spiced meat and pine nuts folded into crunchy filo triangles, tangy homemade hummus, grape leaves stuffed

with lamb and rice and seasoned with dill and lime juice. Nona
had two of every kitchen gadget—blenders, choppers, butter
melters—one in the kitchen and one under her bed.

BIRD BREEDERS WERE PLENTIFUL IN MY AREA. WE SHARED INFOR-
mation and traded birds to broaden the gene pool in our flocks.
Having sought acceptance in a group for so long, I felt sheltered
by these people, who wanted to teach me what they knew. When
Dr. Z started a "flock file" for me at her office, encompassing all
my birds, I knew I'd graduated from dabbler to pro. The whole
enterprise felt important and exhilarating. Each egg represented
a life that hadn't been there before I put the process in motion. It
was an ego-driven venture, for sure, but I learned about life and
love from those birds. Their world was like the human world on
a smaller scale. The mothers defended their babies fiercely, and
the fathers defended the mothers. Sometimes the mothers and
fathers mauled the babies, or each other, and there was no way to
tell in advance which couple would be doting and which would
be deadly. They guarded toys jealously and had frequent infideli-
ties in the large outside aviaries, but the gestures of bonding
between pairs resembled love—protecting the other from inter-
lopers, cuddling and preening, and offering gifts, such as a spinach leaf or a palm frond.

Always, *always*, the birds tried to escape their cages. They
became ingenious at escaping. One little green male, Chicky,
slipped his cage several times by lifting the cage's front door and
squeezing out of the small space. Or, perhaps, he had his mate,
Holly, hold the door up as he unfettered himself of his prison.
Once at large in the bird room, he'd fly from cage to cage and
release as many other birds as he could.

I'd walk into the bird room to find half the birds out of their
cages and Chicky in the middle of it all, delighting in his mis-

chief, hanging on to the edge of a cage, flapping and chirruping wildly. It took me weeks to determine that Chicky was the free-wheeling custodian of the bird room—one day I snuck in to find him in the middle of a jailbreak.

Birds are optimists. When I locked my birds in their cages, they didn't resign themselves to captivity. They didn't fade into a depression so deep that the sky felt like a stranger. Even flightless birds know there's a place for them beyond the chicken wire. It's the birthright birds want more than food, more than love—to escape from the cage, to fly, to soar, to see the earth from the appropriate perspective—above.

Chapter 9

THE FALL I TURNED TWENTY, NONA HAD A SMALL STROKE AND LOST some movement on her left side. Poppy doted on her, cooking and cleaning, doing exercises with her following illustrations on a photocopy the hospital gave him with her discharge papers. She was mobile, but slower.

Several months later, on a Friday night, Poppy called and asked if I could come over and help him with Nona. I was about to leave the house to meet some friends at a party. Perhaps he could call someone else? I was over an hour away. My parents were out and I had no way of reaching them. There was desperation in his voice, but I didn't think whatever was happening could be that bad. If it were, wouldn't he call an ambulance?

At the party, I couldn't shake Poppy's voice. *"Chérie,"* he had said, "I cannot do this myself. I need to get Nona into the car."

I found a pay phone near the restroom of the restaurant, but Poppy didn't answer, so I called my house, and my mom told me that Nona had been taken to Doctors Hospital in Coral Gables. I was confused about the distance, because there were many hospitals much closer, but that's where her primary physician was affiliated.

I teetered into the emergency room in high heels, short skirt, and sequined top, a mint in my mouth to cover the smell of beer, and found Poppy and my parents sitting in the waiting room, gray and anxious.

"Your grandmother had another stroke," my dad said, the rims of his eyes red and wet.

Nona was parked on a gurney in the hallway next to the nurse's station, hooked to machines, clear tubing connected to her in strands, buoying her body on the bed, like she'd sink without them.

"Nona?" I said, peering into her face. I grasped her good hand.

"I never thought I would finish in a hospital," she said in a gravelly voice, tears streaming toward her ears. She was seventy-two. Grandmothers live far longer.

"That's not what's going to happen," I said. "You'll be fine. You'll see." I couldn't understand why the doctors walked around and joked with one another as if no one there needed a miracle.

I stayed the night with her. We were in a low-ceilinged room by ourselves on the second floor, repetitive, disharmonic beeping emanating from every room and bouncing off the concrete hallways like racquetballs. A nurse brought me a reclining chair, but there was no rest. I sat up watching Nona, rubbing her paralyzed hand and foot as if I could shimmy life back into them, like trying to extract fire from a wet stick and a soft stone.

Early in the evening she could still move her fingers and toes a little. As the night progressed, she lost all use of her left arm and leg, and the left side of her face wilted.

I begged the nurses to call a doctor. At three in the morning I called my parents for help. Maybe the "adults" would have more luck conjuring a doctor. My parents came, asked for a doctor, and received the same reply. "She's having a stroke, this is what happens," a nurse said. Researchers were developing thrombolytic drugs to dissolve clots in stroke victims' brains, but those drugs weren't available in 1990. All we could do was wait.

After a few days they moved Nona to the rehab facility in Baptist Hospital, the same hospital where I was born. Poppy would be unable to care for her until she regained the use of her arm and leg. The rehab had a fake supermarket with plastic produce in generous piles and empty boxes of macaroni and cheese arranged on an endcap, and mini shopping carts the patients pushed around as part of their physical therapy.

I overheard my dad telling my mom that a therapist said Nona wasn't going to improve. Weren't the therapists supposed to help her? I visited Nona every day after my classes and wheeled her around the hospital's lake in the sunshine, determined to heal her myself.

"Nicole," she said, tapping her nose, "please tell them to take this out. I don't want this." She had trouble swallowing, so they had pushed a tube down into her stomach through her nose and anchored it there with a large piece of white tape. I'm sure it was uncomfortable and embarrassing. This was a woman who never left the house without copious hairspray, cologne, and rouge on her cheeks. When I wheeled her back inside I asked the nurse if she could have the tube removed.

"That's how we're feeding her, sweetie," the nurse said with a white grin. I thought of my baby birds and how I fed them.

"I'll feed her with a little spoon," I said. "I'll help her, I promise." The nurse smiled again, all teeth and sparkling eyes, and I had to tell Nona there was nothing they could do.

About a week later I drove to the hospital after school wearing a pair of plain white tennis shoes I had embellished with pink rhinestones and gold glitter glue, and topped off with shiny gold shoelaces that formed a giant bow at the top, like a birthday present. Nona would like them.

In the rehab area, my shoes cast rainbows on the walls as the florescent bulbs flashed on the facets of the rhinestones. I was in a good mood, happy to be done with the day and eager to see Nona.

I walked to Nona's room. Someone else was in her bed. I asked a nurse where they had moved her.

"Oh, honey, you'd better call home," she said, rubbing my back, staring at the floor. "Those are some nice shoes."

I called home from the nurse's station.

"Nicole, come home," Poppy said. "Your grandmother is in surgery in a different part of the hospital." I worried when Poppy didn't call me *Chérie*.

"Where? Tell me where she is."

"Come home." His voice trailed off as he handed the phone to my mother. She told me to drive carefully, her voice singsongy and tentative, like she was talking a jumper off a ledge.

"What happened to Nona?"

"Just come home. And drive slow, it's raining."

I knew Nona was gone. She had finished her life in a hospital, as she had dreaded. The automatic hospital doors opened to the outside with a whoosh and the hot Miami air enveloped me like a sickness. I paused outside for a moment and looked around. The lake was a gray scab and the sodium lights cast buzzy orange reflections onto the growing puddles in the drizzle.

I bent down and untied my shiny gold shoelaces, took off my pink rhinestone studded shoes, walked to the trash can in front of the hospital doors, and tossed them into it.

I walked into the house wearing drenched, dirty socks, tracking mud puddles across the slate floor. The extended family— aunts, uncles, and cousins—had gathered in the living room. Blank faces swiveled toward me. I ran down the hall into my room,

Poppy, my dad, and my mom trailing behind me. I slammed the door and locked it. Nona was the first person close to me to die, and I didn't know what came next.

"Nicole, please let us in," Poppy urged, knocking on the door.

"Only Poppy," I said.

"And Daddy," my dad said, tears in his throat. Somewhere in all this I had forgotten that he had lost his mother, a woman he had either seen or called on the phone every day of his life.

I unlocked the door.

THE DAY OF THE FUNERAL, MY PARENTS AND I DRESSED IN BLACK. Poppy wept when he saw us and asked us to change clothes. He didn't want us in black—he'd had a sister who died in Egypt at seventeen, and his mother wore black and mourned for the rest of her life. I changed into a blue skirt Poppy had sewn for me, and a starched white collared shirt. I spent the entire funeral with my head buried in Poppy's jacket. I missed everything except Poppy and my dad scooping dirt with a shovel and tossing it on top of Nona's plain pine coffin. Poppy asked me if I wanted to toss some dirt on it, too, and I declined, trying to push away the giant, burning stone in my throat, and buried my face into his jacket again.

Every time a funeral was held for one of Poppy's friends, or even someone in our family, he always said, "Funerals are sad, Chérie. You are too young for funerals. Do not come." And I didn't, except for Nona's. He instilled in me a strong aversion to funerals—even stronger than our shared fear of flying, ironic for two people who felt a kinship with flying creatures. I didn't know at what age a person was old enough for funerals, because he never told me, but I avoided them no matter who had died, unless I was cornered or guilted into it.

A few days after Nona's funeral, we moved Poppy's possessions from his condo and into our home. He and Nona had been living on Social Security, and with Nona gone, it wouldn't be enough.

Poppy fended off grief by cooking dinner every evening, sometimes two and three dinners a day, putting the next day's meal into the freezer, baked ziti with béchamel sauce, lasagnas, and spinach pies. We ate at the table as a family every night for the first time in many years. Before that, my parents ate together in front of the TV, and my mom kept a plate for me for whenever I rolled in, or I foraged in the refrigerator for myself.

"I like this change of eating at the table as a family," my mom told me privately. "But you have to talk to your grandfather about his food. We're all going to gain a hundred pounds."

It was peculiar not having Nona around. I knew she had passed away, but I couldn't get my head around the permanence of death. Poppy spent most of his time either cooking or shut in his room. My mom said he felt guilty, and that deepened his grief. I didn't know what she meant, and she changed the subject when I asked. I felt guilty, too. I could have saved her. I could have stayed with her twenty-four hours a day, watching, guarding.

Poppy had moved his birds in with us, my babies and grandbabies, and our combined flock grew to more than seventy birds, flying free in one of two outside walk-in aviaries, or living in the bird room in pairs in large cages. We shared bird cleaning and feeding duties. I liked having him across the hall, in spite of the circumstances that had brought him there.

"Did I ever tell you about the sparrow merchants?" Poppy asked one evening as we sat together after dinner.

I shook my head, though he had told me about the sparrow merchants dozens of times.

"I used to sit outside at Café Riche," Poppy said. "Cairo was like Paris then, everyone strolling arm in arm, a beautiful, clean city. The sparrow vendor pushed a metal cart with a cooking grill on top and burning coals beneath. The cart had long hooks on each corner hung with dozens of small cages, each crammed with tiny sparrows, like a hot dog man, but with birds."

At this point in the story Poppy's voice always became quieter and deepened, as if he were revealing the secret to a long-held mystery. "The sparrow merchant speared a dozen brown sparrows alive onto a stick, then roasted them on his coals, plucked off their little feathers, and someone would eat the sparrow kabob for lunch."

This is the part where I gasped and placed my hand over my mouth. "He didn't," I said.

"I swear to you. And every time he passed I bought two cages of sparrows, fifty to a tiny cage, and took them home to your daddy when he was a boy. We opened the cages and let them fly from our balcony, so happy to be free."

"People ate the birds alive?" I asked, horrified again by the story, unable to envision the scene.

"Not alive. Roasted."

"What happened to the sparrows you released?"

"I hope they flew far away."

"What if they didn't?"

Poppy thought for a minute, staring over the waterway through the sliding glass door. "The sparrow merchant would catch them again."

"I'd rather hear about the bird market of Paris. Did Nona ever go there with you?"

"Of course. Your daddy, too. We went every Sunday, crossing the bridge over the Seine on foot, maybe stopping to have an ice cream. Your daddy loved the birds. Why do you think he allows you to keep so many?"

"I don't know."

"Ah! We have found something you do not know. Write down the date." Poppy reached to tickle me and I pushed my chair back on two legs, avoiding his tickling hand by an inch. He pulled my chair back down on four legs, and I laughed.

"Birds are mystical creatures," he said, still holding down my chair. "Did you know that birds are messengers? Doves mean *peace* and bring messages of hope. When a dove comes to you, all possibilities are open."

"What happens if two doves come to you?" I thought about the pair of ring-necked doves who sat together on the asphalt near my car every morning.

"If two doves arrive at your feet you are very lucky. Pigeons are lucky, too. Pigeons mean *safety* and *home*. No matter where you take them, they always come home."

"What do lovebirds mean?"

"Lovebirds mean *love*, *Chérie*. What else could they mean? But you have not seen lovebirds until you have gone to the bird market in Paris. Tremendous colors, a living rainbow of feathers, the best birds you have ever seen."

Part Two

Chapter 10

IN A FLORIDA SUMMER, THERE ARE OPPRESSIVE DAYS AND RAINY days, and days when cookies will bake on the dashboard of a car—but there's no *perfect* day. Perfect days are relegated to January and February, when the tropical thunderstorm pattern fizzles, leaving South Florida cool under cloudless skies. But we had one perfect Florida day the summer I was twenty-two years old: August 23, 1992, the date of my parents' twenty-fifth wedding anniversary. The wind picked up from the east, the palm trees bent their heads west, and the sun steeped everything in golden light. The storm a few hundred miles to the east sucked the bad weather into its whirling eye, leaving us cool, breezy, and flawless.

Hurricane Andrew was coming.

Offshore hurricanes threatened us each year, but the last big one to slam South Florida had been Betsy in 1965. Hurricane Andrew looked like another storm that might choose a different tack, maybe detouring to Cape Hatteras or out to sea. As South Floridians emptied Home Depot of batteries and plywood, I stood outside in my purple bikini cutting coconuts off the palms with a twelve-foot tree saw. They might fly off in the storm and break our windows, and it was my job to remove them while my dad tied my new aviary to our sea grape tree with a long chain. I was into my second Corona and slicked from head to toe with suntan oil.

A hundred yards across the calm, brown water that served as our backyard, at King's Bay Yacht Club, hundreds of sailboats and yachts cruised into the basin like refugees. Their captains lashed them onto docks, the walls of the turning basin, and to one another, hoping the basin would provide a nautical refuge. After a few hours I could have walked from one side of the basin to the other hopping from boat to boat.

I sunbathed on the bow of our little open fisherman, the *Déjà Vu*, as a manatee cow and her baby cruised by, their tails sluicing the water. I leaned over the boat's railing and watched a blue parrotfish picking at crustaceans on the dock pilings. The manatees toured through the boats in the basin, then swam back the way they came.

We watched the hurricane on a small black-and-white antenna television in the kitchen. Hurricane Andrew's circumference was larger than the width of the state of Florida, and meteorologists speculated that its eye winds spun up to 175 miles per hour, with tornadoes inside of the storm gusting up to 206 miles per hour. Andrew had been upgraded from a Category 4 to a Category 5 hurricane. We were used to seeing hurricanes bounce away from us, following the warm Gulf Stream to the north. But I still couldn't understand why we were among the only people in the neighborhood not taking precautions.

"Why aren't we boarding up?" I asked my parents, who were preparing tuna fish sandwiches for lunch. "Should we do something?"

"The lights will go off, maybe a window'll break, and a little water might come in," my mom said. "It's not a big deal. We've seen this a hundred times."

"It'll be fun," my dad said. "We'll light candles and play some games and it'll all be over."

"Tell that to the neighbors," I said. From outdoors came the sounds of buzz saws slicing plywood and hammers driving nails. Poppy walked into the kitchen, concern on his face.

"You're worrying for nothing," my mom said. "Come have a sandwich."

"Should we go somewhere safer?" Poppy said. He and my dad exchanged a few words in French about "the little one" being overly concerned.

"I understand you," I said. They switched to Arabic.

"It's not like we have a lot of places to take a flock of birds and a bunch of cats," my mom said.

"North. Inland. Somewhere away from this thing's path."

"You're a worrywart," my mom said.

On television, people cleared grocery stores of water and canned goods, and the home improvement stores ran out of wood, tape, flashlights, and batteries. The ATMs were stripped of money, the gas stations emptied of fuel. This was bad news because I often let my aging Oldsmobile Cutlass Calais run on fumes. I went out and turned on the ignition, and the low fuel warning light shone yellow.

Back inside, the phone rang and my mom handed it to me.

"I found a baby bird," the male voice said. "I don't know what to do with him." It was my friend Matt, a sweet younger guy who suffered a puppy crush on me, though he had accepted our arrangement as "just friends" and had become one of my dearest confidants. I wanted to date someone older than I was—as most girls I knew did—and I didn't give Matt a chance. He bought me thoughtful presents for every holiday, took me to romantic restaurants, flattered me with kind and heartfelt words. He was cute, too: dark hair and a well-proportioned face, deep-set dark eyes, and long eyelashes. We spent hours hand in hand, walking from frozen yogurt shop to frozen yogurt shop, thinking the exercise earned us giant hot fudge sundaes along the way. We made tie-dyed T-shirts and sold them at the flea market together, and spent long days at the beach tanning and playing in the water.

"What kind of bird is it?" I asked.

"I don't know. Just a brown baby bird."

Had this been an average day, I would have told him to leave it alone if it was fully feathered. Its parents were likely nearby, and it was learning to fly; but it would never survive a storm. I told Matt to bring the bird to me.

I didn't want a North American native bird in my possession, but I had little choice. The Migratory Bird Treaty Act, the breaking of which comes with a fine of up to two thousand dollars and two years in jail, kept most people from capturing songbirds, such as cardinals and blue jays. Matt dropped off the baby bird and rushed home to continue boarding up his house.

The wild bird's alert eyes peered at me from his fragile head. He looked like a woodpecker, but intuition told me he wasn't one. I didn't recognize his species, which wasn't unusual, because I didn't know much about native birds. He had a brown body, a small red crest, and lanky gray legs. I wasn't sure how to care for him, not knowing his species, but I couldn't take him to a wildlife care center with the impending storm and no fuel in my car. Poppy said he didn't know what kind of bird he was, either, and Poppy was superior to me at bird identification. I cooked some hand-feeding formula and offered it to the baby in a pipette. He opened his mouth wide and swallowed the pipette, notably different from how my baby lovebirds ate.

What I didn't know about feeding passerines, the order of birds to which I knew he belonged, could have filled a book back then; but I did know he needed to be fed every couple hours. If the electricity blew, how would I heat the hand-feeding formula? Cold hand-feeding formula slows down a nestling's digestion and can cause infection, even death. Baby birds also need to be kept warm in an incubator, or at least with a heating pad, and I wasn't going to have access to either should the storm take down our power lines. And did he have diseases he could pass on to my birds? There was no way to tell.

Taking care of a bird—any bird—was a welcome duty, but with the hurricane on the way, I needed to move my outside aviary birds into cages inside the house, and try to figure out who the pairs were. If I couldn't tell the individuals apart, I'd have to place each lovebird into a separate cage or they would fight, possibly to the death. There was a lot to do in my avian world. Matt's stepdad, Larry, came by and asked my dad to help secure his sailboat in the basin, and they spent an hour tying the boat down while I safeguarded the birds and my mom dragged our potted plants into the garage.

Sometime in the afternoon the National Weather Service announced emergency evacuation imperatives for neighborhoods in the path of the storm. Our neighborhood, King's Bay, lit up on the weatherman's map. Poppy's friends who lived a few miles inland said we could stay with them, but we couldn't bring the animals.

"I'm staying," I said, as we all sat around the TV in the kitchen.

"Come with me, *Chérie*, we'll have fun," Poppy said. "You cannot stay here alone. Do you trust your Poppy?"

"If I can't take the animals, I'm not going. There's danger coming. Can't you see it on the map?"

"Nicole, we're going and you're coming with us. End of story," my dad said as if I were a child talking about my trip to Narnia.

"We'll be back tomorrow," my mom said.

"Maybe I can siphon some gas from the boat?"

"Marine fuel won't run your car," my dad said. "It's mixed with oil."

I walked into my room and closed the door. The neighbors outside shouted to one another to hurry up. I wasn't angry, upset, or scared. I was resolute. I'd ride it out with my animals. If only a window broke, what was the big deal?

Police cars drove up and down our street with bullhorns blaring. "This is a mandatory evacuation zone," they warned, static punctuating the beginning and end of each sentence. "You must leave your home." They repeated their orders in Spanish.

Two policemen came to the door. Through my bedroom window I overheard them talking to my parents.

"We're making sure you folks are packing up," one cop said, his radio buzzing with garbled voices.

"We're headed to a friend's place in Kendall, but our daughter doesn't want to go," said my mom.

"We can arrest anyone who doesn't leave on a second-degree misdemeanor."

"No problem, Officer, we're all leaving."

My mom appeared in my doorway a minute later. "Did you hear the police?"

"They're not going to arrest me."

"They could. And then what would you do? We'd have to come bail you out in the middle of a hurricane. You can't take your animals to jail, can you?"

She was right. Being arrested would eliminate my post-storm options. I had no choice but to leave and force myself to believe that the storm would exhaust itself over the Bahamas, even if my intuition said otherwise.

I called Matt and asked if I could stay with his family. Matt's family was also in an evacuation zone, but in a non-mandatory area, about half a mile inland and not on the water. I could walk the three miles home from Matt's house after the storm if necessary. His mom, Gloria, said I could bring some of my birds, so I packed my ten youngest lovebirds into a cage, those just starting to eat on their own, along with the wild baby bird in his own small cage.

I rolled a small aviary with ten black-masked lovebirds into our rec room, and stacked the rest of the cages containing peach-faced lovebirds—about sixty birds—onto counters, shelving, and the floor in the bird room behind the kitchen. I always knew Bonk—I could pick her out in a crowd of green peach-faced lovebirds—but her mate, Binky, wasn't as easy to recognize in my hurry netting the aviary birds, so they were separated. I didn't want to risk putting Bonk into a cage with another bird that might hurt her.

I put extra food and water into bowls for Gladys, Emmeline, and Paisley. Not long after Nona passed away, Poppy had found my dear Sylvester, the tuxedo kitty I'd trained to give me his paw and to sit on command, dead in the front yard at just eleven years old. We'd had a cat memorial service, complete with candle lighting and a Hebrew prayer. I missed him.

My baby albums with my infant photos and a curl from my first haircut were near the sliding glass door facing the canal, along with a Tiffany-style stained glass lamp shade Nona had soldered after she retired, so I moved those to the couch for safety. I changed clothes and grabbed an old radio to take with me.

The birds seemed protected in the back room, buffered by the kitchen on one side and the garage on the other. The next-door neighbors had several parrots, and they left them in their home when they evacuated, too.

"You have one last chance to come with us," my mom said. I told her I wouldn't. "I'll leave you the address in case you change your mind. Don't forget to lock the door." She headed toward the car, where my dad was waiting.

"*Chérie*, please come with your Poppy. Do not let me be alone."

"You aren't going to be alone, Poppy. You're with everyone else."

"That does not mean I am not alone."

"Poppy, come on."

"Call me every hour. I will wait for your calls and not sleep until I know you are safe."

Then they left.

My parents believed the storm was a minor speed bump in our day; they left home with no preparations to secure the house, no putting away or taking of valuable and sentimental objects, no thought to the possibility of more than a window breaking. I stood in the middle of the living room, the day still bright, and thought I should stay. I could hide from the police and hunker down in the house to look after the animals; but in the end, I forced myself to trust what my parents said. Matt picked me up in the late afternoon.

I don't know why I left Bonk behind.

MITCH AND BRAD, MATT'S OLDER BROTHERS, WERE BOARDING UP windows and moving furniture into the middle of the living room when Matt and I arrived. Gloria and Larry, Matt's stepdad, kissed me and welcomed me inside. Karen, Brad's pretty fiancée, was there, and Gloria's little Maltese, Goldie, ran around our ankles begging to be held. I placed the cages of lovebird babies and the wild baby bird into the bathtub in a hallway bathroom and closed the door. I figured they'd be safe because there were no windows in that room.

Matt's family loved me and considered me an adopted daughter. With three sons, having her sons' female friends around was fun for Gloria. She came back from every shopping trip with presents for me: elaborate hair ties, shower bonnets, and fancy soaps—girly goodies she couldn't buy for her boys. Larry had a racing sailboat, now moored in the basin behind my house, and Matt and I spent summer evenings cruising around Biscayne Bay on the boat, curled together on the bow, almost in love.

Gloria and I drove through deserted streets to buy dinner. Most of the stores were closed and boarded up, but one fast food chicken place had a long line in front of it, so we parked and waited. The wind trembled every leaf and the sky turned oyster shell gray.

Back at Matt's, we found some board games and puzzles and ate our dinners. The storm appeared and sounded like a normal Miami thunderstorm—thunder and lightning, the wind howling through the space under the doors. Matt and I spooned in his bed and I fell asleep with the warmth of his familiar body behind me.

I woke up alone at midnight in a darkness that felt almost sinister. The power had gone out, and the storm rattled the boards over the windows. I knew Matt's room was an addition to the home, and I believed it was less safe than the rest of the house. I scrabbled my way into the living room by feeling along the walls, following voices and candlelight coming from the master bedroom.

"Matt, you left me in there by myself." I was scared, but when I spoke, my words came out as angry.

"You were sleeping. I didn't want to bother you," he said.

I wanted a drink, but was too self-conscious to ask for one. I sat cross-legged on the king-size bed with everyone else. We listened to the storm, wind and rain and thunder, debris pinging like birdshot against the boards over the sliding glass doors in the bedroom. I tuned my radio to Y100 and we listened to Bryan Norcross, our famous local meteorologist. He was our link to the outside world. The phones had long gone dead.

"It's not the strong winds that destroy windows and homes," Norcross said in his soothing, authoritative voice. "It's the debris that turns into projectiles."

As the wind escalated, huge pieces of debris flew against the house, vibrating the walls. Matt held my hand. I still wanted a drink, but we were huddled in the bedroom, and I didn't know how to ask for alcohol from people who weren't drinkers.

"When we move, you need to move to your safe spot, too," Norcross said from his newsroom, preparing to retreat to a back room with his scant crew. "Examine your house and find a safe place, but don't lock yourself in anywhere, because if the water starts rising you may have to fend for your life."

I squeezed Matt's hand, imagining water flooding the room and wondering how we'd escape, since all the windows were boarded. Wind whistled through every crevice in the house, and I hoped the water wouldn't reach the ceiling. How would Goldie survive? I'd hold the little Maltese above the surface if I had to drown to do it.

At three thirty in the morning, Bryan Norcross and his crew said they were moving to a safer spot inside their studio and that we should do the same.

We didn't move right then, but fifteen minutes later windows shattered all over the house like a series of bomb blasts. We ran into the closet and slammed the door, huddling together and watching the walls sway. I imagined the house peeling apart in the wind. The roof shook and my ears popped. The square attic door above us danced from the pressure building in the house. We communicated with our eyes as objects hit the house and vibrated the floor and walls. No one spoke.

"Do not think that you are in any way safe," said Norcross over the radio waves. "If you have not hunkered down and gotten that mattress over you, friends, this is the time to do it. Get into an interior closet, get a mattress over your head, and wait this thing out."

I clasped my hands over my ears. Larry showed us the pressure lowering on the barometer he had taken off his sailboat. I was thankful to have someone nearby who wasn't panicked. Maybe we'd live through this.

Then the batteries in my radio died.

More crashing sounds and splintering glass and wood, like a demolition crew taking down a building rebar by rebar. I held my breath, listening for my lovebirds chirping, but the storm growled on the other side of the wall, drowning any living voices. I held little Goldie in my lap and petted her, consoling myself.

After an hour in the darkness the storm relaxed, and we left the closet. Bradley peeked outside and reported that the storm seemed over. We opened the bedroom door and walked into the living room, starting to assess the damage in the darkness, when another wall of wind and debris struck the house, and we ran back into the closet. The lull had been the eye of the storm, an eerie break in the calamity, like the bells ringing between rounds in a prizefight. The pressure dropped again—the winds had reversed and grown stronger—and the house shook to its foundation. I waited for the roof to collapse and kill us all.

The hurricane ditched us around sunrise, crawling west to say good morning to Fort Myers and Clearwater. Every window in the house was broken; a foot of water stood in the sunken living room; dirt and debris were strewn all over the kitchen. The pressure had pushed one of the windows from the frame, leaving a large, rectangular gap in the concrete of the house. Cabinet doors were torn off their hinges in the kitchen, and the piles of dishes inside had delicate heart-shaped green leaves stuck between the plates. The baby lovebirds were safe in the bathroom and chirruped when they saw me, clambering to the front of the cage.

We all walked through the space where the front doors had once hung into a hard drizzle and whipping wind under a gray sky. Fluffy yellow insulation and roof shingles of all colors covered every inch of ground, obscuring the distinction between lawn and asphalt. Half a roof sagged on a lawn across the street, and every power line, phone pole, and tree sprawled on the road. A green street sign reading "124th Street" stuck up from the ground where the wind had planted it. We were on 136th Street.

Neighbors paced around in a daze, talking to one another and wondering how we would survive, at least in the short term. We had been shoved back in time: no running water, electricity, or phone service. This was Miami in August and we needed water, at least. Did everyone we loved survive the storm? We had no way of knowing. Cell phones weren't commonplace back then.

I fed the wild baby bird some cold hand-feeding formula. Everything I knew about birds said it was a bad idea, but I had no choice. I needed to return home to assess the situation there, and I thought I'd meet my parents at the house. I wasn't panicked—I was numb.

I told Gloria I was going to walk home, and I wanted Matt to come with me, but they didn't want to let me go. Downed power lines slithered over every street. A neighbor wandering the streets with us agreed to drive me home after I begged for a ride. He pulled an immaculate, shiny black Porsche 911 from his garage, a surreal vision against the backdrop of ruin. I settled into the tan leather seat and we set out on the three-mile drive. We wove around downed trees and cars that looked as if giant hands had picked them up, smashed and twisted them like clay, and then tossed them down again.

We couldn't take a direct route because most of the streets were blocked by mounds of debris, which rose higher as we drove closer to the water, hills of the remains of people's homes. Yachts balanced atop heaps of seaweed and debris on the roads. Furniture was piled on downed trees. Clothing, shoes, bicycles, and toys were scattered across the wreckage. Everywhere people stood in front of what remained of their houses, holding babies, small dogs, and shotguns.

The neighbor stopped his Porsche six blocks from my house because the roads were impassable. He agreed to climb over the debris with me, so we picked our way over large, dangerous piles of rubble, navigating boats and wrecked cars. The neighborhood smelled like sewage and baking seaweed. The unforgiving August sun had returned and was cooking everything it touched.

The neighborhood was so destroyed, so changed, that I became lost on the way to my own house. Not one landmark or street sign remained. Some of the mountains of wreckage were ten feet high, and by the time I approached my block I was dirty and sweaty, scratched on my arms and legs like I'd fought with a cat, and I was bitten all over by giant red ants that had taken over the piles of organic debris. I had little hope that my cats and birds were alive.

The terrain was bizarre, but the strangest aspect of the scene was the absence of birds. No birdsong; no fluttering and cawing; no flocks lighting on power lines. The bird world—so much of my own world—had gone dead.

Of the hundreds of boats that had been secured in the basin, only a handful remained, including Larry's sailboat. It no longer had a mast, but there it was, tied up by a single line to our dock. The rest of the basin was all brown water, sunken boats, and wrecked docks. Two boats slumped in our front yard, a Chris Craft open fisherman named *Daddy's Girl* and a small dinghy with the name *Patience* stenciled in cursive on its stern. Our boat was gone. Our sea grape tree had been severed at the base. The coconut palms had lost their heads. The neighborhood's old shade trees were lying on their sides, their gnarled roots reaching ten, fifteen feet into the sky like giant, bumpy dinner plates.

I climbed a mountain of seaweed on my hands and knees, wheezing from the exertion and filth, and listened to the silence. There was not even the buzzing of flies.

Then, as I approached the house, the sweetest sound breached the silence: birds. Lovebirds. They were alive. I ran the rest of the way, jumping over downed power poles, furniture, and hunks of rooftops.

I didn't need my house key. The house no longer had doors. Inside were mountains of seaweed, hundreds of live crabs, and dozens of dead fish. The fish littered the living room. Our furniture was no longer in its place. Couches were outside on the patio and shoved into the kitchen. A pile of debris reaching almost to the kitchen ceiling blocked the door. A water line on the wall in the living room from the storm surge was seven feet above the floor, well over my head. The shell of our house was there, the foundation was there, but the guts were flood ravaged and shattered, and the sewers had backed up, coating the floor with fetid muck.

I picked my way to the blocked bird room, sneakers sinking into the gunk and making a sucking noise each time I lifted a foot. The little aviary I had wheeled into our rec room was intact, and all ten black-masked lovebirds had survived—the water hadn't risen as high in the back rooms.

The bird room was another story.

There was Bonk, clinging to the front of her cage. She rattled the cage door and chirruped at me. The other cages were scattered everywhere, sodden and broken, and in them my other lovebirds, dozens of them, were dead. The cages were bent and mangled, the bodies of the birds soaked in salt water, dark and limp. One yellow lovebird flew around the room and I grabbed her. She bit me hard, and I couldn't blame her.

I overturned a bent cage and pulled out a young seagreen lovebird named Lala. Her body felt cold and wet, her wings drooped, and her head slumped. Birds vibrate like a Bach fugue through tiny subwoofers when you hold them. Maybe it's their souls that reverberate with such force, and her soul, her song, was gone. I had intended to put her in the aviary as soon as her wings grew out; she had never experienced flight. I cried and held her to my chest.

I pulled out Birby, then Bunky, and another, Batty—Bonk's children, all silly names starting with the letter "B"—until I had a dozen dead birds cradled in the front of my T-shirt: babies that Bonk had fed, nurtured, and loved.

Chicky, the little renegade who released my other birds from their cages, was dead inside his nest box with his mate, Holly, and their eggs that would never hatch. They had hunkered together as the water rose.

Bonk's mate, Binky, was also dead. Bonk must have known he was gone, because she clung onto the front of the cage and shrieked over and over—to me, perhaps, but also to him. Lovebirds stay next to the bodies of their fallen mates, even when danger is nearby. I stood in the rubble, arms full of dead birds.

I can imagine only so far into their storm. The water rose and the birds stacked at the bottom climbed as high as they could before the water overtook them. Then the cages floated and the ones stacked on top tumbled into the water, giving the birds a few moments to find a way to keep from drowning. From the appearance of objects in the room, the water hadn't become violent there—it had just lapped in and drowned them.

In the back room, six of the sixty birds I had placed in there had survived. The water had risen to the halfway point of the cages on the counter, sparing the birds in them. Miami Bird, the red-lored Amazon parrot, was salt-water stained from the chest down, one-half of her a dark algae green instead of iridescent lime. She whistled and cooed and her irises pinned in and out with excitement at seeing me, and she lifted a foot and waved, as I had trained her. I bawled. What would I have found had her cage been situated a few inches lower?

None of the survivors—sixteen lovebirds and Miami Bird—had food or water. The salt water had washed away those supplies.

There was no way to find seed or fresh water. The neighbors had parrots, so I ran to their house. All their birds had survived, but they didn't have fresh water, either. The neighbors said they'd look after my birds as best they could until I returned for them.

While I inspected the damage to the rest of the house, Gladys and Paisley emerged from the rubble, yowling, raked fur wet with mud and standing on end. The nails on their front paws were raw and meaty, scraped down to the bone. They must have clawed all night in the water to save their lives. I found my Baa-Baa on the floor of my room covered in sewage, the ratty blue security blanket Nona had given me when I was three. I gathered the cats into the wet, stinky blanket and carried them out of the house. Paisley had been a wild cat with a mean streak, but she grasped me around the neck and kissed my face and wouldn't let go.

I called for Emmeline, the mute, but she didn't appear.

The guy who had driven me home didn't want me to sit in his new Porsche with a dirty blanket and two filthy cats. I cried and stood in the middle of the street, cradling my terrified cats, looking and feeling like a refugee, too numb to plead or fight, and he relented. I didn't know where my parents were or if they were alive, and there seemed to be no working phone for miles.

Matt's family bustled around the house, sweeping and tidying despite having no windows, doors, or running water. They were trying to put things back in order. But I couldn't put my world back together with a mop and broom. It seemed to me that I had killed my birds, my friends, as if I had plunged each of them into the water and watched them drown. I stepped into the five inches of rainwater still in Matt's sunken living room and knelt to wash my sewage-covered hands and face. I stared into my reflection, muttering and rocking back and forth, repeating that I had killed them, that it was my fault. I slapped the puddle so I wouldn't have to see my face.

Gloria tried to pull me from the water, but I resisted. She pulled me to my feet and shook me. It was like one of those moments in a movie where someone slaps the hysterical person, and I think it almost came to that. I screamed until a stranger, a man, walked into the house through the nonexistent front door. We all stopped talking and turned to look at him.

"What's going on here?" he asked cautiously. "I heard yelling."

Silence hung in the air for a moment, and then I rambled about not knowing where my parents were and about the dead birds and cats, and I don't remember what else, but little could have made sense to him. I was crying the whole time.

"I have my wife and daughter in our truck and we have a stop to make, but you're welcome to ride with us," he said. "I'm a minister, it's OK."

Gloria said she would care for our cats and my ten young lovebirds until I could return, and I left with the stranger, carrying nothing but my grief and a wild baby bird.

WE DROVE FOR FOUR GRUELING HOURS AROUND THE RUBBLE, THE remains of the city, forging through dangerous intersections without traffic lights, past businesses and homes razed to the ground. I glared out the window, unable to answer even the simplest of questions. I was numb, but I didn't feel shot up with Novocain—I felt like the needle.

I reached my family and managed to thank the minister for the ride. A fallen tree blocked the driveway to the house where my parents and Poppy had spent the night, and they couldn't move their SUV. I told them about our house, the wreckage, the yachts standing on end on top of homes, the dead birds, and about our missing cat, Emmeline. There was no horror on their faces, no sign that they understood what I had seen. I wept, Poppy holding me to his chest.

Trees and power lines were down in West Kendall; there was ample roof damage, and screened-in patios were demolished, but my parents and Poppy hadn't been smacked by the hurricane's full force. They had slept through the storm. They had no phones or electricity, but they had cold running water.

I wanted a shower and needed a drink; but since Poppy was there, I managed only the cold shower. By the time we reached our house the next afternoon, the smell was twice as bad as it had been the day before. The sewers in the neighborhood had backed up even more, and the fish and crabs in the house had rotted in the heat. I gagged as we picked through the rubble. My dad cried at the wasteland that had once been our home. We had nothing: not one item of clothing except what we were wearing, not a piece of furniture, not one old photograph.

We mucked around in the sewage on the bottom of our rooms and found a precious few items to keep. Poppy found some of his old coins. I found a pair of silver heart-shaped earrings. A few objects on my highest shelf were still there, too, including Bonk's first eggs and the globe Nona and Poppy had given me for my ninth birthday. I found photos of other people and a suitcase that wasn't ours, and there was a soggy dining room chair in the hallway that no one recognized. I figured most of our furniture was in someone else's house, as if the entire neighborhood had held a giant involuntary swap meet.

We drove from hotel to hotel in North Miami Beach and found a vacancy in a squat, '50s-era motel. There was still no electricity, but we had hot running water, and the hotel bar had warm beer. After three days, the Army cleared the roads enough for us to drive to the site of our former home to retrieve the surviving birds. Emmeline was still missing.

We had a friend in Fort Lauderdale with a large aviary on his screened porch, and he agreed to take my birds until my parents and I found a place to live. I opened their cages inside the aviary and turned on the hose and sprayed them down. They drank and bathed in the fresh water. They had full flight and freedom, but they didn't leave their water dishes for nearly half an hour. Bonk dipped her head into the water and soaked herself in it, wetting her chest and wings. The salt water must have burned their eyes and skin. I hadn't spent more than a couple days away from Bonk in over four years, and now she would be without her mate and without me.

The grief pressed on me, waking up, sitting at lunch, going to bed. It had roots, and bloomed into a quiet suffering I couldn't express. I wept for days and couldn't stop. I drove to the wrecked house every day and scanned the sky, wishing that some of the birds had escaped.

My grief branched further and breached all my walls when I realized Emmeline was truly gone. I walked through the neighborhood asking everyone if they had seen a black and white fluffy cat, and I yelled her name for hours. Despite being mute, she could hear.

"I think Emmie was washed out to sea," my dad said, hugging me. "You aren't going to find her."

Ten days after the storm, on the last day of searching for Emmeline before I'd desert that house and never return, in the last five minutes that I would ever be in that place, my parents waiting in the car, I lifted a fallen closet door and found Emmeline curled in a hollow underneath it, unable to escape from the pocket in the rubble around her. She looked at me and mouthed a huge, mute meow that would have been audible across the street had she been able to make a sound. I plucked her up and rubbed my face on her dirty fur. We all cried when I stepped into the car with her, grateful for one small miracle.

I didn't see Bonk for more than six weeks. My car survived the storm except for a shattered windshield and a beating to the paint job, but my parents sent it to the body shop, and I had no transportation to visit the birds. We moved from hotel to hotel in North Miami Beach with the cats, away from the trauma of the storm, but still without electricity.

The wild baby bird Matt had found languished and became quiet. He stopped crying and begging for food. The inside of his mouth became sticky and he couldn't perch anymore.

Maybe I wasn't feeding him enough, or perhaps not feeding him his native diet? My life was so unsettled and my environment so changed, I didn't have the resources to find out what kind of bird he was, or take him to the veterinarian. He wasn't weaning onto anything I tried—seed, fruit, suet, meat. Nothing worked. We visited one of my parents' friends in north Fort Lauderdale who happened to have a few books on wild birds, and I found him in an illustration after an hour of searching.

The little guy was a red-whiskered bulbul, *Pycnonotus jocosus*, native to China, India, Pakistan, Thailand, and Burma. In the early 1960s, fewer than ten red-whiskered bulbuls had escaped from a rare bird farm in South Miami and established themselves in the subtropical environment. In the next ten years, their population rose to about 250 and kept growing, adapting to South Florida and thriving on wild figs, jasmine, and the berries of the Brazilian pepper tree, also called the Florida holly. Bulbuls weren't native, but people didn't consider the pretty little birds pests, and put out feeders to attract them. Their range in South Florida remained small, mostly in the Kendall area of Miami, where they were first released. That area was now destroyed.

Did I have possession of the last red-whiskered bulbul in South Florida? Did fate somehow put us together: this rare bird and a bird girl? I had to find a way to save him—I would have tried regardless of his species, but now it was critical. I borrowed a phone book and called a wildlife center, but they were filled to the rafters with orphans after the storm, so they gave me the name of someone who handled wild birds, who gave me the name of someone else.

Finally, a sympathetic wildlife rehabilitator agreed to take him. The lady wasn't going to be home when my mom and I dropped off the bulbul, so I put him in a carrier and set him on her doorstep. I called her to ensure that she had found him, and she said he was fine and eating a lot of fruit. He was a little dehydrated and seemed to have a lame foot, but he was hungry and perking up, and was going to be OK.

I didn't call the lady again. I hoped she released the bulbul so he could find another surviving member of his species and start the rare colony again. Since bulbuls weren't native, she wasn't required to release him. Maybe he never flew free again. Birders say there's still a population of red-whiskered bulbuls in South Florida, in the same area where Matt found that little guy. Maybe that bird helped to rebuild the foundation of his species in the one small area in North America they called home.

Chapter 11

AFTER HURRICANE ANDREW MY MATERIAL POSSESSIONS CONSISTED of a beat-up gray Oldsmobile Cutlass Calais; one boom box radio; two changes of clothing; a pair of cheap silver heart-shaped earrings; Bonk's first egg; my blue security blanket, BaaBaa; and the globe Nona and Poppy had given me when I was nine. With a little FEMA relief money, we bought beds and linens, a dinner table, and some silverware. Friends in Broward County gave us clothing and shoes.

I'd lost the encyclopedia set Poppy had bought me as a kid; I'd lost love letters from various boyfriends and crushes over the years; I lost my baby pictures and the blonde curl from my first haircut; I lost my record album collection; I lost three gold rings Nona had given me, and my prom dress, my high school yearbooks, and a black duck stuffed animal Poppy had bought me when I was five. It was missing a flower on its head, and I had insisted he buy it for me out of fear that if I didn't take her home, no one else would.

I learned that stuff is just stuff. But the birds weren't just stuff. Losses from the hurricane devastated Poppy, too. Looters had stolen his locked safe before we reached the house, and he had kept his most prized possessions there, a treasure trove amassed throughout a lifetime of traveling: gold coins, old foreign money, photos, and other irreplaceable keepsakes, including Nona's wedding ring, the one she had fought to keep when fleeing Egypt.

My parents, Poppy, and I moved into a sunny three-bedroom rental house in north Fort Lauderdale, ten minutes from the beach. Our new home had a screened-in patio with limestone floors and sliding glass doors surrounding a kidney-shaped heated pool on three sides.

I started my flock again with lovebirds, pairing my current birds with new mates. While we were separated, Bonk had married a cute little blue-pied lovebird named Sweetie who had also lost his mate in the hurricane. Sweetie was one of my favorites, a precious guy who hadn't been hand-fed, but allowed me to hold him. Bonk and Sweetie settled in by going to nest and tending to eggs.

Each new bird or clutch of babies fledging from the nest made me feel a little high. The world dropped away, and I was washed holy: Saint Francis in short-shorts. I had to be above reproach in everything I did, to ensure my animals were the best cared for animals in the world. I had failed during the hurricane, and I wouldn't allow that to happen again.

Bonk's babies with Sweetie were unlike her babies with Binky, which had been carbon copies of her: green, with a peach face and cobalt rump. Sweetie had something spectacular buried in his genetics that mingled well with Bonk's genes, because their babies emerged in a palette of lovebird mutations: silvers and cinnamons, cinnamon pieds, blue pieds, jade pieds, and seagreens. I often wondered if Bonk might have been "cheating" on Sweetie in the new aviary I built, which housed all my remaining lovebirds. Whatever the case, whenever I heard her hatchlings cry for attention, I couldn't wait to spy into the nest box and see what miracles Bonk had created.

I accrued not only dozens more lovebirds, but also noisy sun conures, nanday conures, mitred conures, and jenday conures—South American birds three times the size of the lovebirds, and far more raucous. I acquired red lorikeets and Australian cockatiels in a medley of mutations; *Brotogeris* canary-winged parakeets; Indian ringnecks; budgies, finches, and canaries; *Poicephalus* parrots; two more red-lored Amazons, one as a mate for Miami-Bird; diamond doves and button quail; clamorous Quaker parrots and Hahn's mini macaws; and a *Chapmani* mealy Amazon named Sam someone had given me, an endangered species and the biggest—and fattest—Amazon parrot I'd ever seen.

I'd catch Poppy spooning baked ziti into Sam's insatiable maw, or my dad handing him almond after almond. If we didn't "invite" Sam to have dinner with us, he'd scream until one of us ferried him to his spot at the table. He loved lasagna and pasta—anything with red meat sauce—the food falling from his bottom beak as he ate; he'd just dip his head back into his plate and shovel it all back in. The corners of his beak were often stained pink, and he had garlic breath. He loved vanilla ice cream cones, too, and consumed foods I'd never give my other birds—Sam ate like a person and demanded to be treated like one. My mom spent hours bribing Sam with grapes to say "I love you," which he learned to say on cue.

Most of my birds came to me as unwanted pets that needed new homes, gifts from friends at the bird clubs, or trades I made using my baby lovebirds. I acquired birds in a frenzy, not thinking, moving on autopilot to reharmonize my shattered avian world.

These weren't the only birds in my life—every dusk, a flock of dozens of feral nanday conures landed on the screened patio to talk to my nanday conures, screeching and shrieking. Sometimes, a wave of Quaker parrots arrived at dusk, too, and pushed my birds into an uproar of squawking and screaming that continued until the sun succumbed to the stars. My dad complained about the nightly ruckus, so I conducted a "parrot non grata" patio watch in the evenings, shooing the wild birds back into the trees with a broom.

My daily tasks were performed by rote, caring for the birds and continuing college classes; but at night, when the world quieted, my thoughts abused me in a voice I didn't recognize. *You killed the birds*, it said. *You killed the birds*. I couldn't argue with it and I couldn't shut it up. *You killed the birds*. I couldn't shake the images of their wet, drowned bodies, imagining the surge overtaking their cages, and their first—and last—breath of water, suffocating them as they panicked, clinging to the last pocket of air as their cages sank beneath the surface. I'd come home from class and curl in a ball on the floor, drinking cheap port wine, rocking and apologizing to the dead birds over and over until I passed out. Often, I'd crawl into my closet and close the door, curl as small as I could in the corner, knees to chin, and drink from the bottle until the bad thoughts ceased. Sometimes I woke up there.

Our rented Fort Lauderdale house was three blocks from Baja Beach Club, thirty thousand square feet of wall-to-wall toned and tanned flesh and tequila shots. I hadn't been to many nightclubs before, having spent most of my twenty-first year preoccupied with birds. The club represented a new world for me.

Fort Lauderdale sweltered, but one foot inside Baja's double doors and the chill prickled the hair on my arms. The club smelled like suntan oil, liquor, and oranges. The gym-bodied male bartenders wore only tight black shorts, and had their names written on their naked pecs in black Magic Marker. The female bartenders wore bikini tops and short-shorts, and girls in G-string bikinis sat in front of aluminum horse troughs filled with ice and beer, selling brews and multicolored liquor shots in test tubes.

All of the bartenders wore whistles around their necks, and tossed handfuls of napkins into the air when someone ordered a "body shot," which meant that a patron was allowed to lick salt from the chest of a male or female bartender, have the bartender pour tequila down his or her throat straight from the bottle, and take a lemon from the bartender's mouth. Every now and then, a siren sounded and a bartender stood on the bar to aim a toilet paper machine gun at the crowd. In the bathroom, girls vomited and snorted cocaine off toilet seats before boogying back to the dance floor.

I hid among the chaos and danced drink in hand on top of the huge elevated speakers, wanting nothing more than numbness among the excess. If I danced alone on the dance floor, within minutes I'd have a guy grinding behind me and a guy grinding in front; when I danced on the speaker, the guys watched me but left me alone.

Scantily clad ladies didn't have to wait in line, and a sixteen-dollar Cherry Bomb was equal to five drinks, because it came in a large plastic beach bucket. Tuesday at Baja brought two-for-one drink specials, and Thursday was ladies' night—girls drink free until midnight. I'd stop drinking at about three so I'd be slightly less drunk for the three-block drive home at four a.m. After a while I realized I could drink until closing if I stumbled home on foot, so I'd either walk to the club or ditch my car in the parking lot and pick it up the next afternoon.

Despite the almost daily drinking, I could still wake up and tend to the birds, commute to college over an hour each way, and write papers on Shakespeare's tragedies or Robert Frost's early works. Keeping all those birds and drinking the way I did was expensive, so I took a part-time job in a pet store at the mall underneath the Baja Beach Club, working the register and selling pet supplies and animals.

The job was dangerous because I brought loads of animals home, all sorts of unwanted pets people brought into the store—a giant white rabbit named Hoppy that I found in the back room in a trash can, several turtles, and a one-eyed hamster named Euripides who had a giant wound on his head that cost me fifty dollars at the veterinarian's office. This was in the first couple weeks.

No matter where I traveled or for what reason, if I saw a bird store I had to pull over. On one stop in Miami's Little Havana neighborhood, I walked into the bird store to find a large fish tank full of fluffy yellow chicks among the usual finches, canaries, and parakeets. I stuck my hand into the middle of the tank and caressed the hatchlings, their warm, fuzzy bodies wandering over my palm like silk. One of the chicks stood taller than the others by more than a head. I watched him for a while as he milled around with the others, pecking at the cracked corn in the feed dish.

"How much are these?" I asked the clerk. He looked at me and blinked. *"Cuánto es?"* I tried.

"Dos dollars," he said, holding up two fingers.

Two bucks, and the big chick was mine. The man plopped him into a brown paper lunch sack, stapled it at the top, and handed him to me. He peeped inside of the sack the entire way home.

I placed him with Hoppy the rabbit in a large cage, which looked more like a giant dollhouse painted orange and pink. I knew they'd be fine together. When Poppy came home from the racetrack I showed off my new chicken, rubbing the bird on my cheek as Poppy reached to pull my hands away from my face.

"That's not a chicken," Poppy said, unconcerned that I was now bringing home barnyard animals.

"How is he not a chicken?"

"That is a turkey, *Chérie.* You see this?" He touched the fleshy tab growing at the top base of the bird's beak. "Turkeys have this, not chickens. What are you going to do with a turkey? Is he for Thanksgiving?"

I clutched the fluffy bird to my chest, now noticing the growth near his beak. "No, come on," I said.

"You are now the proud mother of a turkey, *Chérie*. Congratulations."

Tom the turkey grew fast, and ran around the house after me with twice the devotion of a golden retriever puppy. White feathers emerged from his fluffy body when he became a gangly teenager. I allowed Hoppy the rabbit to bound around the house, too. He stood on two feet against the kitchen counter as my mom made salad in the evenings and gave him vegetable trimmings.

On a routine trip to Dr. Z's office, I mentioned that I had an adolescent turkey in the house.

"You have a *what*?" she exclaimed, turning to me, a pen dangling from her fingers.

"A turkey," I said.

"Absolutely not. You can't keep fowl and parrots together. The diseases are crazy. I swear if you don't get rid of that turkey, I won't treat another one of your parrots, ever. Get it out."

"Are you serious?"

"No turkeys."

I left her office dejected, but Dr. Z's word was avian gospel to me: I'd have to rehome Tom. I called a few petting zoos and found one that would take him. The lady seemed experienced with birds, and placed him in a big cage with an adolescent duck. At least he'd have a bird friend.

Despite Tom's departure, our house remained a menagerie as I kept collecting. I grew mealworms in the kitchen pantry so I could feed them to some of the birds who needed insects. When the mealworms matured from the larval stage, they turned into big black beetles. I spent at least three hours a day tending to the pets, and Poppy and I fell into an unspoken routine of cleaning and feeding.

One day, Poppy pulled me aside on the patio as I hosed down the bottom of the birdcages.

"Nicole, I need to talk to you," he said. We sat down on two floral patio chairs. "I do not sleep at night when you are out. Can you please come in earlier? I worry so much for you. There are hunters out there."

It didn't occur to me that I was disrupting Poppy's life.

"*Chérie*, you are still naive and young. You come home all hours of the night and I think you are drinking."

"I am not," I countered, feigning offense. "I'm almost twenty-three. I have nothing else to do here."

"I understand. I was once your age. I like to have fun. But sometimes I see you leave your car somewhere else and you concern me."

I decided to take Poppy to Baja Beach Club to show him that it wasn't a dangerous place. On Wednesdays they had a happy hour buffet. The spread was a Fourth of July party meets Cinco de Mayo: hamburgers and tacos. The crowd was sparse, the lights bright, and the music not as loud as it would be later. We walked up the tall staircase to the double doors and I winked at the doorman as he handed us four free drink tickets. I walked Poppy to my favorite bar and we ordered soda. We filled our small plates and sat in a booth on the far side of the club, where black lights shone on fluorescent murals and made our teeth glow purple.

"This place is nice," Poppy said, eating a taquito. "We should do this every Wednesday." So we did.

I still attended all the local bird club and society meetings, and I started writing and mailing the newsletter for one of them under the pseudonym "Lolita Lovebird." I became an expert in lovebird genetics and color mutations, and received at least a dozen phone calls every day from people asking questions about breeding birds, bird behavior, and bird problems. I called one of my mentors when I didn't know something, usually Dr. Z. *Bird Talk* magazine—the gospel in birds and my *New Yorker* with feathers—hired me to write for them after I had submitted dozens of unsolicited articles.

People gave me more unwanted birds, including a large blue-crowned Amazon named Lolita who had become homeless when her human owner died, and who trilled her own name in a singsong voice, over and over, endearing herself to everyone in the house.

"She is so cute," Poppy said, handing Lolita an almond. "But I think she is saying *lorita*, not Lolita."

"Why do you think that?"

"*Lorita* is 'little parrot' in Spanish," Poppy said, studying her. "Maybe we should teach her to say 'fat bird' instead."

Someone brought me a double yellow-headed Amazon parrot after his dog had torn off one of the bird's wings. I took the parrot to Dr. Z to see if "Captain Hook" could be saved. She said someone had rubbed a salt poultice into the bird's wound, so she cleaned it, added a thousand dollars to my already lofty vet bill, and then wiped my bill clean because she was touched that I'd been taking in unwanted parrots.

"Why don't you find a man and have some kids?" she said, handing me Captain Hook's carrier. Dr. Z had just returned from maternity leave after the birth of her first child, and showed me photos of her adorable newborn. "Kids will cure you of this bird mania."

"I have *feathered* kids. *Fids*," I said, looking into Captain Hook's carrier, the frightened one-winged bird huddled in the back.

"You look terrible," she said, scrutinizing me up and down. "How are you going to find a husband in this condition? Preferably one who doesn't like birds."

I might have had bird poop on my shirt and a little in my hair, but "terrible" seemed an excessive estimation. "This from the avian vet who owns only one bird," I said.

"I can't stand birds anymore. Birds are driving me crazy. And *you're* driving me crazy. Get out of here. Stop taking in all of these birds." She waggled a finger at me and I hugged her.

———

MY PARENTS HAD LEFT THE CAR DEALERSHIPS AND WERE BACK IN the garment business by my early twenties, making screen-printed T-shirts with tropical birds and fish on them for hotels and cruise ships. They let me sell the shirts at bird fairs and expos to support my bird habit, which had grown to well over a hundred birds.

I'd done well at a pet expo in Coconut Grove one weekend and was packing my unsold T-shirts when I overheard the people in the booth next to mine complaining that they hadn't earned a dollar. I'd been eyeing a Meyer's parrot that rode around on the lady's shoulder for the entire three days, and when I heard them talk about needing to cover the booth, I asked about him. The lady said he was four years old and his name was Jesse. He was a deep shade of brown, almost dark gray, with a bright yellow head and a turquoise chest. I had other Meyer's parrots, but they were breeders, not tame, and they were also terrible parents who always ate their eggs or killed their babies. I took Jesse onto my finger and he lowered his head for a scratch.

"How much?" I asked her.

She paused. "You can have him for two hundred and seventy-five dollars."

"You're going to sell Jesse?" the breeder's husband asked her. "Seriously?"

"We haven't sold anything else," she said.

I had sold enough T-shirts at the expo to not haggle about the price. Jesse perched on my shoulder the whole drive home. I didn't know it then, but I had just bought myself a future lifeline.

Careening on avian autopilot with no brakes, I also brought three huge macaws into the house: a blue and gold macaw named Comet, whom I bought as a baby from a breeder friend; a green-winged macaw named Sonnet who was seized in a legal situation, auctioned, and given to me; and a vicious scarlet macaw named

Satan-Bird-From-Hell who had become useless to his breeder after he killed three females. These birds were beautiful, like avian supermodels, but louder than all the others combined.

If the house had been noisy before, these guys cranked the volume to *deafening*. My parents and Poppy liked the macaws—the birds were flashy, intelligent, and status symbols—and my mom had a particular relationship with Comet, so for a few months no one said anything about their noise. Everyone loved Jesse, not only because he was sweet and marched around like a confident little Napoléon, but also because he was *quiet*. My mom didn't even care that Jesse hung out in the kitchen and chewed up her cookbooks.

Bird noise is cumulative—it might be manageable for months, even years, but one day the chirping, squawking, talking, and twitting breaks someone's sound barrier, erasing whatever noise tolerance they'd built. *I* didn't hear the birds anymore. A macaw could scream in my ear and it wouldn't register; but my dad didn't share this quality, and we started fighting about the conures, Amazons, and macaws. He even blamed me for the feral colonies of parrots that visited us. I was forced to thin the noisier birds from my flock. Each bird I rehomed tore at the thin scabs that had formed over the dozens of bird-shaped wounds I'd suffered in the hurricane, and alcohol was the only thing that alleviated the sting.

On the Fourth of July, I walked to Baja Beach Club to meet two guys and a girl I had been hanging around with there. I found them at one of the back bars, already drinking. I rolled up to the bar, greeted them, and ordered a margarita on the rocks. I shot that and ordered another.

We walked toward the side bar, where it was a little quieter. I took the lead, and on the way stumbled into a girl, spilling part of her drink. Cold liquid and ice splashed onto my sandals. I looked into her face, waiting for a reaction.

"You spilled my drink, bitch," she yelled over the music. Her red mouth formed the word "bitch" in slow motion, her hoop earrings swaying against her cheek as she swiveled her neck in my direction.

I could have said, "Excuse me" or "I'm sorry." But I stared into her eyes, stunned, waiting for her to speak again. Instead, she pushed me. Without thinking, I shoved her drink into her face. She dropped her glass, shattering it on the floor.

In seconds, she and three other girls jumped on top of me, punching and kicking. I gripped one girl's long, red hair, pulling her toward my face while her friend pounded on my back. The redhead laughed.

"I didn't do anything to you!" she yelled, smiling like a carnival barker. I released her hair. They were punching me, and I was throwing punches, too, though my punches were not connecting. Two bouncers squeezed through the crowd and pulled us apart. I had two seconds to breathe before they pushed us back together for round two. I thought bouncers were supposed to stop fights and kick out the perpetrators, but these bouncers wanted more of the show. Punching, slapping, kicking. I couldn't get my bearings: faces, lights, the floor, the ceiling, each a flash, like wayward images in an ill-edited movie. The bouncers pulled us apart again, and the girls disappeared into the crowd. No one asked me if I was OK, nor did they ask me to leave.

I looked for my "friends." They stood with their backs to the wall, drinks in hand—watching, frowning. I stumbled over to them, wiping my face.

"Why didn't you do anything?" I yelled over the music. I was livid. And drunk. And my shirt was torn.

"You can't do that stuff when you're with us," one of the guys said. "I'm on probation, I can't get into that."

"I've got a weapons charge pending," said the other guy. "You need to be more careful."

The girl sipped her drink from a red straw. They walked me to the bathroom. My nose gushed; my right eye was red, the skin puffing taut like a grape. I found a cop sitting on a stool at the back door to the club.

"Some girls beat me up," I told him, pointing in the direction of the fight.

"You can leave through this door right here," he said, pointing to the metal door leading to the fire escape stairwell. No expression, no concern.

"Can you do something about it?" I screamed over the music.

"You're free to leave," he said.

I found my supposed friends again and asked Mr. Weapons Charge to take me home. I was too scared and shaken to walk home alone.

Poppy stepped out of his room wearing a long red nightgown as we rambled into the house. My parents were away on business, the one blessing of the night. I sat at the dining room table and cried as Poppy and Mr. Weapons Charge tried to console me. Poppy filled a plastic bag with ice and I held it against my eye as I sagged at the table.

"I should go," said Mr. Weapons Charge. "You want to walk me out?"

Mr. Weapons Charge leaned out of his car window and grasped my forearm. "You shouldn't invite people like me into your house," he said. "Don't do that again."

"What do you mean?"

"Just don't." He released my arm. "You don't know what someone can do." He drove off into the night toward Baja Beach Club. I never saw him again.

I woke up with a black eye, my nose swollen shut, and bruises on my ribs and back. I looked at my reflection in the mirror, expecting to be horrified, but I smiled. I gave that girl a few good smacks, didn't I? Then I thought about Mr. Weapons Charge. Poppy was right. I was more naive than I'd thought.

Chapter 12

ON MY TWENTY-FOURTH BIRTHDAY, POPPY CALLED ME INTO THE yard and handed me my birthday dove. Of course, I knew by now that this "dove" was really a white pigeon, but we pretended it was the international symbol of peace anyway. I cherished our birthday ritual, but this year I didn't want to release the "dove."

"I'll keep her," I told Poppy. I wanted to protect the bird— make sure she had a safe and happy life. I didn't want her to become a star in the sky, floating in the emptiness with nowhere to perch.

"Let her fly, *Chérie*," Poppy said. "She wants to be free."

I felt sad holding the bird in my hands. I had anticipated her, and prepared a large flight cage for her new life with me—food and water already filling the dishes.

"You have so many birds." Poppy put his arm around me and gestured above us. "Look at the sky, how big and beautiful. Let her go."

I knew once I opened my hands, I couldn't take the gesture back. I had so many bird-shaped scars on my heart, and I didn't want another. I thought I might die if something as gentle as the breath from free-flying bird wings touched me.

"Where does my birthday dove go?" I asked Poppy, as I did every year, but this time I said it as an accusation, not a question. I wanted him to tell me the truth for once, that the dove wasn't magic, that she was a fragile soul whose life could be extinguished with far less trouble than it took to create her.

"To the stars, of course," he said. "You can see her every night if you want."

"I don't know if that's true anymore." I rubbed the warm bird onto my cheek and Poppy gently pushed my hands down.

"You are too old now to believe your Poppy?" He gazed over the water, his face sad, eyes cloudy.

I breathed deeply, closed my eyes, and launched the dove into the air with both hands. Her wings whistled as she left us, arcing to the right in a big curve and disappearing over the rooftops. I felt relieved, which surprised me. Something inside me healed a little.

"Happy birthday, *Chérie*," Poppy said, clapping his hands. "May you have many, many more."

WHEN OUR LEASE RAN OUT ON THE RENTAL HOUSE IN FORT LAUDER-dale, my parents, Poppy, and I moved to North Miami into another rental, away from Baja Beach Club, but closer to Florida International University's north campus, where I continued taking creative writing classes after graduating with a bachelor's in English and a minor in philosophy. Our new rental house sat on a wide waterway, similar to the waterway behind our hurricane house. Gone was the safety of a grassy backyard. I'd gaze over the waterway and imagine water breaching the seawall, forcing its way into the house with intent to drown us.

On the positive side, the house had a large, sunny patio, perfect for the birds, and a living room with an alcove, where I placed the cages for the larger birds. I had grown up in Miami, and was happy to be back.

Moving away from Baja Beach Club was good—staying out all night drinking was dangerous and a pathetic distraction from what I felt was truly important: the birds. I had acquired a prolific pair of rare—at the time—yellow Fischer's lovebirds. The hen laid ten to twelve fertile eggs in a clutch, when the typical lovebird clutch is between four and six eggs. A pair on its own can't raise that many babies. Most lovebirds have three to five babies hatch per clutch, a manageable number for good parents. Eggs are laid approximately two to three days apart, and the mother begins sitting on the eggs to incubate them after the third egg is laid, give or take an egg or two. The first eggs cool and stop developing until the mother resumes incubation.

For a lovebird pair with ten viable eggs, the first baby could be more than seven days older than the last baby, leaving the last babies at a great disadvantage. A seven-day-old lovebird is enormous compared to a hatchling, and most of the little ones are crushed to death, cast aside, or buried. In the case of a clutch of five viable eggs, I'd pull the first two babies from the nest and start hand-feeding them about the time the fourth and fifth babies hatched, giving the entire clutch a chance to thrive.

It's also challenging for the parents to warm a clutch of ten to twelve eggs. Some of the eggs will break, be pushed aside, or not be warmed as well as the others. If I wanted this pair's babies to survive, I would have to pull the first six eggs from the nest and incubate them myself. I invested in a forty-dollar Styrofoam incubator from a feed store and learned how to use it.

I hadn't wanted to incubate eggs, like some of my bird-breeding colleagues did. I liked having the parents raise the babies until they were about two weeks old. I'd pull them from the nest and hand-raise them after their eyes had opened.

The working theory in bird circles is that the babies should see the parents when they first open their eyes. The babies bond to humans better this way. Many parrot species are genetically programmed to move away from their family when they reach maturity so they can breed within a diverse genetic pool. If they stay nearby, they risk breeding with a sibling or other relation. Birds raised with their parents first, then a human, are affectionate and sweet. Lovebirds incubated and hand-fed from day one are tame, but tend to be willful and bratty toward humans, and are fierce breeders, unafraid of human hands.

After pulling the eggs from the nest, I gently pencil marked an X on one side of each egg and an O on the opposite side, then placed them all onto the fine wire mesh at the bottom of the incubator. I poured some water into the water channels below the grate to keep the eggs' environment humid. I turned the incubator to 98.6 degrees Fahrenheit and let it heat slowly, so the eggs didn't experience thermal shock.

Every couple hours, when the eggs were young, I'd open the clear plastic hatch at the top of the incubator and turn the eggs halfway from the X side to the O side, and later, from O to X, and later another quarter turn, and so on. The developing chicks' circulatory systems require the eggs to be turned, and this also prevents the chicks from sticking to the eggs, which would kill them. If I wasn't home to turn the eggs, Poppy did it for me.

I ordered a candler for ten bucks from an ad in *Bird Talk* magazine. A candler is the avian version of an ultrasound machine. This one was a small, thin flashlight with a long, flexible neck and a pinpoint of cool light at the end. All eggs appear the same on the outside; but with eggs, as with romance, the inside makes all the difference. Placing a candler onto an egg gives an X-ray view into the hard womb.

Infertile eggs are usually lemony yellow inside, called "clear" in bird-breeding terminology. The yolk might be darker, but for the most part, nothing of interest is happening there, and nothing ever will.

The beginning of a fertile egg has a black pinprick inside. Clear eggs were disappointing for me, but that one black spot represented a bit of hope, a speck full of possibility.

As the embryo develops, red veins spider out of the black spot and grow over the inside of the egg's shell like a vine taking over the side of a building. An air cell at the large end of the egg expands, creating a hollow space between the material inside the egg and the shell. Within four days, the veins would lead to a murky spot within the egg—the developing baby.

By now, the chick would have a beating heart. In two more days it would have legs and wings, and by nine days it would start to resemble a bird. I couldn't see this inside the shell—just a spot becoming darker and thicker.

Sometimes the eggs would develop a hairline fracture and I'd cautiously paint clear nail polish over the crack to seal it and keep bacteria from entering the egg and killing the baby. I tended to the eggs as vigilantly as a mother bird.

By day twenty, the air cell would draw down, indicating healthy chicks inside the eggs preparing to hatch. Some chicks kicked inside their shells, sending the eggs rolling all over the incubator, restless to hatch.

Sometimes the chicks didn't kick inside the egg, and I questioned whether they were still alive. At a late stage, the candler showed just a dark, unmoving mass inside the egg. Dr. Z told me that you can tell if a chick is alive by floating the egg in water, so I filled a bowl with lukewarm water and placed the questionable eggs inside. Within a few seconds the eggs bobbed up and down, doing laps around the bowl, the living chicks inside gathering the strength to pip the shell.

Somewhere between day twenty-one and twenty-four, my lovebird eggs woke me in the middle of the night. The eggs were cheeping. I hadn't known that eggs talked. I picked them up one by one and found that two of them were crying with a volume usually reserved for birds, not eggs. I placed them back into the incubator and hunched over it all night, staring through the plastic door until past dawn, as the first chick used its egg tooth—a small, sharp, temporary triangle of bone on its beak—to pierce the egg, and struggled to force itself out into the world, with nothing but the power of will, one chip at a time. It was the most amazing enterprise I'd ever seen, like stillness and ecstasy in a boxing match.

Dr. Z told me not to help a chick hatch unless it seemed in trouble, so I resisted the urge to pick at the eggs with a toothpick, which I had been instructed to do if a chick didn't hatch within a few hours of starting—and which I'd do many times in the future. Hatching looks grueling, but it helps to develop the chick's neck muscles and respiratory system.

Over the next few days, all six of the eggs hatched into squirming, wriggling pink babies. I placed them into a plastic bowl with paper towels in the bottom so they wouldn't hurt themselves on the incubator's wire grate as they hatched, and I raised the incubator's temperature to 100 degrees Fahrenheit—the babies needed extra warmth to dry. They all had egg sacs attached to their bellies, where their belly buttons would be if they were people, kind of like placentas; the egg sacs fed them for the first two hours of their lives. Once the egg sac dried, I had to start feeding them myself.

The newborns needed to be fed every hour around the clock for the first two days, then every two hours for the next four days, then every three hours for the week after that. Parrots are "altricial," helpless when they're born, eyes closed, dependent on their parents—or me—for survival, unlike chicken and duck chicks, which are "precocial," born with eyes open and the ability to walk and find food.

The first feedings consisted of one drop of slightly warmed

Pedialyte, and after that, Pedialyte mixed with a smidge of commercially prepared hand-feeding formula. I was delirious after a few days of little sleep, but had to set my alarm every two hours to wake up and feed the babies, and couldn't leave the house for more than an hour at a time. One of my friends at the bird club was incubating birds at the same time, and we joked about the Dunkin' Donuts commercial running at the time where the groggy baker stumbles out of bed early in the morning and slurs, "Time to make the doughnuts." We'd say, in the same intonation, "Time to feed the doughnuts." I'd fall back into bed until I had to wake again in what felt like a nanosecond.

Watching the "doughnuts" grow was the real miracle. After a few days I removed them from the incubator and placed them in a plastic container with a heating pad beneath it. They morphed from uncoordinated pink squiggles to blind, prehistoric-looking creatures sitting up in their paper towel nest, gaining control of their necks and feet, helpless changelings growing at an astonishing pace. Their eyes opened at about two weeks, first one, then the other, and I welcomed them to the world and told them I was their mama.

Around this time I pulled their six siblings from underneath their parents. Pulling the babies gave the parents a break. Laying and incubating eggs and raising young is a hard job, and it can deplete the parents' resources and the calcium in the mother's bones.

The first time I pulled babies from the nest I thought it was cruel, but the other bird breeders at the club said the parents soon forget about the babies, and that did seem to be the case. After a few minutes the parents behaved as if the babies had never existed, but I wondered if that was what we wanted to believe. We'd never know what kind of panic the mother felt entering her nest and finding her babies missing.

The parent-raised babies were larger, and their growth

seemed more advanced than my hand-fed babies, though they were about the same age. I decided to incubate only when necessary, when parents had too many viable eggs, or were known to break their eggs or kill their babies.

I was exhausted by the time the Fischer's babies were on four feedings a day at about four weeks; I couldn't handle back-to-back incubation. I needed time off until the next batch—and I needed a drink—so I took the prolific parents' nest away. The hen laid an egg in her food dish, so I moved the pair to a cage with a wire bottom so they couldn't access paper anymore, which they used as nesting material. I put the egg into the incubator in case it was fertile.

Without Baja Beach Club around the corner, I didn't drink as much as I had in Fort Lauderdale. At least, not at first, though I thought about alcohol all the time. I also didn't want a repeat of the bar fight. I'd glimpsed something in myself I didn't like that night: alcohol could control me.

But my resolution to lighten up on the drinking didn't last. I met a writer/bartender in a fiction-writing workshop who asked me on a date, and we quickly became a couple. I'd sit at the outdoor bar in Coconut Grove where my new boyfriend worked and he'd mix drinks for me I'd never tried. I had my first chocolate martini. No more margaritas for me. Tequila equaled bar fights and the disintegration of control. Now I was a vodka drinker, along with beer and wine, both of which could barely be considered booze.

I fell in with a group of writers who felt like real friends, including the handsome poet Richard Blanco, whom I met in Campbell McGrath's poetry workshop and would become my closest friend. We'd bond over poetry, martinis, and nights on South Beach, cruising Collins Avenue in his convertible white Mazda Miata with the top down.

A couple of the other writers bartended, too, and my writer/

bartender boyfriend and I would score free shots all night. I discovered that drinking was cool if you were a writer. All the great writers were lushes. I took pride in it. The more I drank, the better a writer I'd become. It had worked for Ernest Hemingway and Dylan Thomas, right?

One night, early in my relationship with the writer/bartender, sleeping off a couple pitchers of beer, a strange noise rose in a dream and I tried to push it away. I didn't want to float to consciousness, but the noise roused me. It was coming from the incubator. Cheeping.

I peered inside the incubator. There were two babies. Was I still drunk? There had been *one* egg from the yellow Fisher's pair. The top and the bottom of one egg were on the incubator's grate, along with two pink, wriggly chicks. I'd had twins. They were tiny—much smaller than regular babies—but they were complaining loudly and performing somersaults.

I didn't even know that lovebird twins happened. I couldn't wait to call my friends from the bird club and Dr. Z. I raised the temperature in the incubator, fed the babies a drop of Pedialyte with an eyedropper, and nestled them into a cup of paper towels. I set my alarm clock for one hour.

My alarm rang in what seemed like a minute. Time to feed the doughnuts. I opened the incubator and found that one of the babies was still alive, but the other had perished in the hour I'd been asleep. I checked the incubator temperature. I'd done everything correctly. I examined the dead chick, and found a layer of skin stretched over each of his eye sockets. He hadn't developed eyes.

I cradled the dead twin in my hand, tiptoed to Poppy's door, and knocked gently. He cleared his throat and turned on his nightstand lamp as I entered his room.

"Poppy, I had twins, and one of my birdies died." I was speaking like a little girl.

"What, *Chérie*? What time is it? Are you OK?"

"My baby is dead."

Poppy peered at the chick in my hand and propped himself up on the headboard. "You are sad for this baby?"

I told him I was. He patted his bed and I sat down beside him.

"You are like a farmer, *Chérie*. On a farm, many animals die. You cannot cry for each one." He held up both of his hands, palms facing the ceiling. "*Merci, mon Dieu*, thanks to God for taking this baby instead of one of us."

I hadn't thought of myself as a farmer. The idea intensified my sadness. I didn't share Poppy's practical nature. I mourned each death equally. I'd had many unfortunate deaths in my flock and cried for each one, but this was the first death from my incubator. This one felt even more personal.

"What do I do now?" I asked Poppy, staring at the tiny dead baby in the middle of my palm.

"We will deal with it tomorrow. Go back to bed, you must be tired."

The next day I found a limestone rock to use as the baby's marker. Poppy and I dug a tiny hole and gave the twin back to the earth. Poppy said a prayer in Hebrew as I placed the rock over the baby's grave. I had an aversion to human funerals, but felt that animal funerals were important.

The other twin thrived. I named her Little Miss Mango because when she feathered out her colors resembled the tropical fruit: yellow body tinged with green, and a red beak, which she wielded as a weapon in one moment and kissed with gently in the next. As her personality emerged, she showed herself to be a sassy creature—smart, fiercely loyal, and affectionate. She grew into one of my best friends, like Bonk: invaluable and irreplaceable. Twins from one egg must happen as often as two moons around one planet, which is to say *it happens*, but no one I knew had ever seen it before.

Chapter 13

WHEN I APPLIED TO NEW YORK UNIVERSITY IN THE SPRING OF 1995, I never believed I'd be accepted, but I was, and in late summer, my writer/bartender boyfriend agreed to drive me to New York City so I could begin graduate school in creative writing, with a poetry focus. I'd had terrible grades in high school and not much better at Miami Dade Community College, but they had improved once I took a few English classes at Florida International University. I think the weight of the graduate application rested on my writing sample: ten pages of poems, mostly about birds. I wanted to study at NYU because of Sharon Olds, a poet whose work explored depths I also wanted to plumb, a soft-spoken woman who penned dark, sexy, semiconfessional free verse pocked with curse words. I was twenty-four, and this would be my first foray into living as an adult in the real world.

I packed the rental car to the roof with black plastic bags filled with clothes and linens, and a giant cooler and boxes filled with food. I was afraid I wouldn't be able to find food in New York City and I'd starve before classes began. I brought dozens of cans of tuna, chocolate and granola bars, Cup Noodles, cereal, and beef jerky—as if I were going camping in the mountains for months. My dad chuckled when he saw the car. He promised me there was food in New York, but he couldn't convince me to leave anything behind.

Pets weren't allowed in the graduate dorm, so my mom and Poppy said they'd care for the birds while I was gone. I removed all nest boxes and anything else that would prompt breeding. My mom requested that I thin my flock, so I reluctantly rehomed some of the birds, my brood winging from my grasp again. I said a special good-bye to Bonk, telling her to be a good girl, kissing her all over her beak and head, and begged Poppy to pay special attention to her.

A few hours before my departure, Poppy walked into my room and closed the door.

"You are my hope, *Chérie*," he said.

"I know, Poppy."

"Call me every day. Do not talk to strangers. The world is a hard place for a sensitive girl. There are hunters out there."

"I know, Poppy."

"You can come home any time you want if you do not like it."

"I know, Poppy."

"You know everything, *Chérie*."

"I know, Poppy."

He grasped his bushy eyebrows at the outside edges and curled them upward.

"Don't do that!" I said, and squealed like I was eight years old.

He grimaced, formed his hands into claws, opened his eyes wide, then stepped toward me with a zombie's gait. I screamed and leapt over the bed, tore open the bedroom door, and ran across the house, Poppy right behind me. I flung myself on the couch, where he cornered me, and the tickling commenced.

"Be careful," Poppy said, hugging me. Poppy pointed at my

writer/bartender boyfriend. "Drive slow. You are carrying precious cargo."

I waved at my parents and Poppy, and kept waving as we rounded the block and they disappeared from sight.

"You can stop waving now," my boyfriend said as we pulled north onto U.S. 1.

By the time we crossed the Mason-Dixon line, we had decided to loosen the binds on our arrangement, realizing that thirteen hundred miles would eventually rend the delicate fabric of our relationship, which was knit more with the threads of loneliness than with strands of anything as strong as love.

MY FIRST DAY IN NEW YORK CITY, MY FIRST MOMENT AS A REAL ADULT in the real world, I sat on my narrow dorm room bed and, instead of chirping, whistling, and screaming, I heard my own thoughts in chaotic layers, each like a line on a graph. On one line I was elated to be on my own. On another line a voice said that I hated it here and I'd fail at whatever I tried. Another reported I was thirsty, and another said I'd be killed in a random act of violence. Another played the chorus from ABBA's "Dancing Queen" over and over.

The worst line told me to jump out of the window. My twenty-fourth-floor dorm room had a north-facing window overlooking Midtown, including the Empire State Building, a million-dollar view of Manhattan.

Jump out the window, the voice insisted. *Jump out the window. Jump out the window. Jump out the window.*

I opened the window wide and wondered how the dorm could allow the windows on the high floors to open all the way. I could hang one leg over the sill, then the other, and push off, flying for one pure moment until the ground caught me in its unforgiving arms.

I decided to wander around my new neighborhood near Murray Hill and drown my anxiety with vodka. A drink would smooth out the ruffles. Hallelujah.

My parents had told me New York City might be overwhelming; instead, I found its street life exhilarating, a new metaphor waiting on every corner. The city's frenetic energy tamped my racing thoughts, and I could concentrate instead on people arguing on street corners and pigeons gathering to peck more holes in a bagel. My neighborhood smelled like curry, and the air was engaged with wailing ambulances.

On my very first day in my new 'hood I found a liquor store and bought a bottle of vodka and a green glass gallon of cheap port wine. Back in the dorm, my suite mate was unpacking her boxes. She was a pale, slight girl from Yale working on a PhD in medieval studies. I offered her a drink and she declined, so I closed myself into my room and started on the bottles.

A few days later I attended my first poetry workshop with Sharon Olds. I made friends in class and we drank at the Cedar Tavern on University Place, or in the dark bars lining Second Avenue and the Bowery. I made friends in the dorm, too, and we drank in the evenings. My writer friends and I enticed strangers on the street to play Red Rover with us. We held hands in a circle around the giant cube at Astor Place during a lunar eclipse and sang '80s rock tunes. We traveled toward Avenue C to the Nuyorican Poets Café most Wednesdays and Fridays to drink and rate the poets reading in the slam, or read our own work and hoped not to be heckled.

Poppy and I spoke on the phone almost every day. He told me about his wins at the racetrack, his backgammon games with friends, and his walks on the beach near sunset, playing paddleball with Canadian tourists. My mom placed the phone near Bonk's cage during each call, too.

"Hi, Bonky! I love you!" I'd yell into the phone, clicking and whistling to her. I hoped she knew I was on the other end, though I doubted it.

Still a pet store junkie, I stalked the pet stores in my area to check on the well-being of the birds, like the undercover avian police. I found a sick lovebird in a chain store on one of my rounds. Employees in these stores typically don't know the difference between a bird and a shoe, so when I asked about him they didn't have any answers. He sat on the bottom of the cage, puffy, sticky, and ruffled.

I bought him, then snuck him into the dorm and called Dr. Z.

"What did I tell you about going into pet stores?" she asked. "You can't control yourself."

"I know," I whined. "But I have him and he's sick."

"I'll mail you some medicine and write it in your flock file. And don't tell anyone I'm sending you medicine. It's illegal."

"I won't," I said, relieved that I'd saved this bird, who looked like Bonk but was not as friendly.

"You need to find a husband," Dr. Z said. "I'm going to find you one, because you aren't doing a good job by yourself."

"I'm working on it." I'd been on a few dates, but nothing had stuck.

"Work harder."

The medicine arrived a few days later, and my new lovebird friend, Guillermo, perked up and became bright and mischievous. I'm sure the other residents heard him chirping, but no one reported me. He lived in my room, chewing my books and inspiring my poems.

I was turning in papers and poems on time, and even teaching a few days a week at a preschool in Union Square, but one night after a few martinis, I alienated my poet friends by insisting that someone carry my backpack because my shoulders ached. After no one volunteered, I screamed at them and hailed a cab, never to speak to most of them again.

A voice still nagged me about the hurricane birds, reminding me that I'd killed them, urging me to step off the ledge of my dorm room's window. Only a giant glass of port wine at the end of the day silenced that voice.

I didn't realize it then, but daily drinking was manipulating my brain chemistry and damaging my central nervous system. I overreacted and took everything personally, from critiques on my poems to someone stealing a cab. I believed that if I felt angry, sad, or slighted, I'd feel that way forever. If something was unbearable, in my skewed thinking, it would be unbearable in perpetuity. I woke Poppy at all hours of the night, in tears on the phone—about stomachaches, the cold dampness outside, and the fact that I missed him.

Once, after a rain shower, I saw a rainbow in the clouds over Queens, and the sight made me shrivel into a corner and cry, so hurt by its beauty and transience—in a moment, it would be gone, and I couldn't reason that it was just the effect of light on water. When I saw someone eating an ice cream cone, especially a child or an old person, I'd weep in public. The ice cream cone was a fleeting pleasure. Soon the old person would be dead. And the child was naive to the hideousness of our ultimate fate. If I ever saw Poppy eating an ice cream cone again I'd turn to ash and blow away. I didn't share any of this with anyone. I knew it was crazy.

During my first-year holiday break, my drinking leveled off. Happy to be with Poppy and the birds, I drank far less. After the break, I returned to NYU to study with Galway Kinnell, a handsome Pulitzer Prize winner with a slight Irish brogue who wrote about practical things with such dexterity that they became almost occult. My drinking increased, as did my mood swings and irrational thoughts. The voice in my head beckoned me to take the big leap and fly through the twenty-fourth-floor window.

My second year at grad school, I was a resident assistant, a gig that came with a private dorm room in an undergraduate building in the heart of the East Village and five meals a week in exchange for playing "dorm mom" to the students and throwing pizza parties. I took poetry workshops in the evenings with Galway Kinnell and with Bill Matthews, another quick-witted poet I admired, and I drank to excess every night after class, sometimes by myself, sometimes with the underage sophomores who lived on my floor. My outsides appeared normal, but my mind frayed with each drink like silk in a washing machine. I bought a large aquatic turtle in Chinatown, named him Swimmy, and kept him in a giant plastic bin filled with water. This quiet friend reminded me of what I desperately wanted—a hard, protective shell.

Chapter 14

WHEN I ARRIVED HOME FOR SPRING BREAK DURING MY SECOND YEAR of graduate school, I found Bonk sitting on the bottom of her cage, feathers fluffed. She waddled to the side of the cage to greet me, chirping, whistling, and clicking as usual, but she didn't look right; she was too puffy and a little dirty. Healthy birds keep their feathers clean. Her belly was distended and she had gray discharge on her vent.

"How long has Bonk been like this?" I asked my mom.

"Been like what?"

"Bonk is sick," I told her. "Can't you tell?"

"I guess I couldn't. She seemed the same to me."

I called Dr. Z and Bonk and I were in her office within half an hour. I was distraught.

"Bonk is egg-bound," Dr. Z said after examining her.

"Oh my God, she's eggnant," I said. *Eggnant* is the colloquial term for avian pregnancy. "She's eight years old and I haven't set her up for breeding in a long time."

"They can breed at this age in good condition," she said.

"I know, but I didn't want her to try."

"Too late for that. She's unable to pass the egg. It might break and fester, which, you know, could be fatal." Dr. Z told me she'd do an egg-arian section and that I should go home. There was nothing I could do. She'd keep Bonk for a few days.

I waited by the phone, nervous, thinking about Bonk's drowned babies and how much she had endured in the storm. I wondered if she remembered watching the water rise, immersing her mate and children. I poured myself a huge glass of wine. Poppy walked into the kitchen, and without saying a word, took the glass from my hand and poured it down the sink. Before I could protest, the phone rang.

"I removed the egg, and that went fine," Dr. Z said. "But I found cancer in Bonk's uterus. It looked like bright orange granules covering the inside of the organ. I'd say she has three to six months to live, if that. I'm truly sorry. Just make her comfortable."

I told Poppy the prognosis.

"Bonk is in the hands of God, *Chérie*," he said. "We will light a candle for her tonight and say a prayer."

I snuck the bottle of wine into my room and finished it. That night, after the candle and a prayer in Hebrew for Bonk and all our dead, I didn't sleep in the bed, but instead curled up on the floor with no blanket or pillow.

When I picked Bonk up the next day, she hopped onto my shoulder, put her beak into my ear and ground it back and forth, whispering to me in a language I understood.

"I'm glad to see you, too, Bonky," I told her.

At home, she hopped into her cage and curled her head down so Sweetie could preen her. Bonk seemed fine. I didn't believe Dr. Z's prognosis. Bonk would survive because I'd will it so.

WHEN I RETURNED HOME THREE MONTHS LATER, BONK WAS healthy, fat, and shiny, her personality as ebullient as ever. But

Poppy had changed. He had been an active retiree going to the racetrack with friends, and now he didn't want to leave the house. He sat in his room, manifesting only at mealtime. He didn't want to spend time with me, and I felt insulted, like I'd done something wrong, but he wouldn't give me the details. No beach paddleball, no horse racing. We were like strangers, and I had to leave for New York soon.

"Poppy, do you want to go to the movies with me, or maybe get some ice cream?" I asked one drizzly afternoon, standing in the doorway of his room.

"Not now, *Chérie*."

I stared at him from the doorway. He gazed at the television. I charged across the house to my room and slammed the door. He had to have heard it. I paced the room, reeling from the dismissal by the one person in the world I thought would never reject me.

Two days before I left for New York, I cajoled Poppy into a walk around the block. Two Rottweilers in a backyard attacked their side of a fence as we crossed the street. They barked and snarled, and Poppy was so startled that he fell down and hit his head on the sidewalk. I rushed to grab his arm and pick him up, but he was seizing, his eyes blank, jaw clenched. Within a few seconds he blinked, his body relaxed, and he sat up.

He brushed himself off, looking dazed. I took his hands and pulled him to his feet.

"Those bloody sycamores," he growled, wiping his hands on his pants, squinting at the dogs, which were panting and wagging their stubby tails behind the fence.

"What just happened, Poppy?"

"I fell."

"Yes, but you blacked out or something, like a seizure."

"I am fine," he said, rubbing his head.

"Are you sure?"

"Of course I am sure. Do you believe your Poppy?"

"I do, but that didn't look normal."

He stared at the dogs and limped a few feet away from them. "Those are bad dogs."

We ambled home, his hand on my shoulder, my arm around his waist.

At dinner, Poppy relayed to my parents the story of the dogs barking and him falling, but he left out the part about the seizure. I took his lead, thinking that if he didn't think it was a big deal, I wouldn't bring it up, either. I agreed the dogs were bad, and offered that the owners probably were, too, though I didn't believe so about either.

The next day, my parents left for the Bahamas on a work trip to sell T-shirts to a resort there, leaving Poppy and me alone. I found him in his bedroom in the afternoon seizing on the bed, froth around his mouth, eyes rolled into their sockets so that only the whites showed. I called 911.

In the emergency room, they took him for an MRI. A young doctor showed up several hours later and told us there was something on the scan—he wasn't sure what it was, but it was likely the cause of the seizures. He gave us a business card for a neurologist and told us to call the doctor on Monday.

I reached my parents and they ditched their trip and rushed home, and I postponed my travel back to New York a few days. They took Poppy to the doctor. My mom found me in my room and motioned for me to sit on the bed.

"Your grandfather is very sick," she said. "He has a tumor in his brain."

I waited for her to explain, but she paused and we both looked at each other. Was she waiting for me to speak? What could I add to this terrible news?

"A tumor," she said again.

"They can fix it." I knew sometimes these conditions were treatable.

"We're going to try. Talk to him. Be positive."

I padded over the cold tile floor to Poppy's room.

"*Chérie*, come here," he said. I sat on the edge of his bed and took his hand.

"Poppy, are you OK?"

"I am OK, *Chérie*. You are not allowed to worry. Promise me."

"What's going on?" I said, thinking I'd hear a more favorable answer from him.

"The doctors found something, but I am fine. How are you, *Chérie*?"

"I'm worried about *you*."

He touched my cheek and smiled, and I felt better.

"You are my hope," he said.

"You are *my* hope," I said back.

My dad told me later that Poppy had been having seizures for several weeks but hadn't told anyone. It started when he brushed his teeth one morning—his jaw clenched around his toothbrush—and instead of investigating it, he just stopped brushing his teeth. Maybe he was embarrassed. He mistrusted doctors. When he was in the army in Egypt, he had been diagnosed with a spot on his lung and given six weeks to live. He left the doctor's office and decided to heal himself, eating oranges and fresh fish and indulging in fresh air and sunshine. That was more than forty years ago. He'd had a mistrust of doctors ever since.

A few days later, while I was packing my suitcase for the trip back to school in New York—Bonk on my shoulder, jumping into my suitcase to inspect my clothes—Poppy appeared in the doorway.

"Do you have to go now, *Chérie*?" he said as I zipped my suitcase. "You can take some extra time?"

"If I don't go back, I'll be in big trouble," I told him. "I'm already here longer than I was supposed to be."

Poppy's face was drawn. "Be careful, *Chérie*. I worry about you. Call me every day."

A few days after my classes resumed, my mom called with news. The tumor was growing. Poppy had seizures daily. My mom said the doctors were figuring out their next move. Poppy was only seventy-eight years old, and people lived to be over a hundred. Why not Poppy?

My mom put Poppy on the phone. He said, "*Chérie*, tell me something good."

"I'm making a lot of friends." I muffled my mouth with my old blue blanket, BaaBaa, so he couldn't hear me crying. The heat kicked in from my floorboard radiator and I flinched at the sound, a loud tick and a hiss. Bonk and the other lovebirds chirped inside the long pause on the phone.

"Where there is life, there is hope," Poppy said.

IN THE THREE WEEKS I WAS IN NEW YORK, MY PARENTS CLOSED ON A house in an upscale neighborhood in south Fort Lauderdale, a three-bedroom split-level situated on one of dozens of canals spidering through Lauderdale Isles, inland enough to be safe from a storm surge in a hurricane, but still with ocean access. Their garment business had taken off, and they were doing well. The house was bordered on the sides with pink bougainvillea and a sloping front lawn lush with St. Augustine grass. Royal and cabbage palms lined the quiet neighborhood, and many of the neighbors had xeriscaped the fronts of their houses, landscaping them with native trees and plants, banyan trees hanging with Spanish moss and large air plants growing in the y-shapes where the branches met the trunks.

My mom picked me up from the train station.

"Don't be surprised by your grandfather," she said in the car. "I'm warning you. Poppy has changed a lot."

"What do you mean?"

"We don't have drinking glasses because he broke them all," my mom said. "We had to buy plastic tumblers."

I tried to imagine Poppy flinging glasses across the room.

"He can't hold anything in his hands anymore. And don't be shocked at how he eats. The food falls out of his mouth."

"I don't understand," I said.

"You will. Another thing." She paused and sighed.

"What?"

"The neighbors down the street have a big white dog, and I guess Paisley got into their yard and the dog disemboweled her. They found pieces of her."

"Way to break that to me gently." I had picked Paisley the cat from a Dumpster when I was fifteen, her eyes barely open, and nursed her with a tiny bottle and canned milk from the pet store.

"I know you and your grandfather have the superstition about an animal dying to save a person. Maybe Paisley died for Poppy. I thought about that when it happened."

I stared out the window at the palm trees in the road's median. "Could be," I said, but I thought, "Yes, that's it. Paisley traded her place in the world for Poppy to stay. *Merci, mon Dieu*, thanks to God."

I walked into the cool house, with its white tile floor and huge sliding glass door overlooking a sailboat across the canal. The house had vaulted wooden ceilings and a covered patio deck for the birds. Gladys and Emmeline greeted me at the door, Emme swiveling through my calves, Gladys yowling for head rubs in her characteristic Burmese fashion. I wondered if they understood that Paisley was gone.

Poppy was resting in his new room at the top of the stairs. He sat in bed, propped up with pillows, staring into space.

"*Chérie*, you are home!" he said when he saw me, reaching out his right hand.

I hugged him and sat on the bed. The left side of his face drooped and he was unshaven.

"I am better now that you are here."

I held his hand and tried to think of something to say. I was angry. I wanted to run downstairs and lambast my parents for not taking better care of him. Instead I told him about my trip and my imaginary friends at school. He smiled and seemed relieved to know I was happy. But I *wasn't* happy—I was furious. I know now that some people hide their elderly away in nursing homes, send their sick grandparents to care facilities where they die alone, that it's hard to watch a loved one disintegrate, and that's what my parents had chosen to do—the hard thing. But not having witnessed his gradual dismantling, I thought Poppy's condition was borne of neglect.

Before dinner, my dad helped Poppy down the stairs and into a chair at the dining room table. My mom filled up his plate. He held his fork in his fist like a shovel. Most of the food slipped off his fork before it reached his mouth. When it landed, he chewed awkwardly, and most of the food fell back onto the plate. It was ghastly to watch. My parents went on eating as if this weren't happening.

After dinner, as my dad helped Poppy up to bed, I cornered my mom in the kitchen. "How can you sit there and watch him eat like that?"

"He doesn't want help. We tried. Your grandfather is a proud, independent man."

"You can make the decision to help him. He has a brain tumor. Don't you think that's affecting his decision-making process?"

"You act like we're not doing anything." She was rinsing dishes and placing them into the dishwasher, the plates clanging against one another like cymbals.

"Fix this."

"How do you want us to fix it, Nicole?"

I wanted to say that we should take him to Dr. Z, a doctor I trusted. But Poppy wasn't a bird.

THE NEXT DAY WE DROVE POPPY TO A NEUROSURGEON'S OFFICE. WE sat in a small, sterile room while the doctor examined Poppy's MRI, then examined Poppy. He told us that the MRI showed a large tumor, about the size of a tennis ball.

"We have two choices," the doctor said. "We can be aggressive and operate to try to remove the tumor, or we can do a biopsy and use a new laser knife technology to blast the tumor, depending on what kind of tumor it is. I can't know the nature of the tumor, benign or malignant, until I either perform surgery or a biopsy. I'll leave the room so you can discuss it."

"I will not be butchered," Poppy said as the door closed behind the doctor.

"I vote for removing the tumor," I said, holding up my hand.

Poppy and my dad started speaking French, something about doctors always wanting to cut. When they launched into English again, Poppy said he would concede to the biopsy. He didn't even want to do that, but we all felt he needed to take an action.

After we returned home, Poppy called me into his room. "*Chérie*, please open the top drawer," he said, gesturing to his nightstand. "There is a book I want you to read."

I pulled out a small red-and-black hardcover journal with the word *Record* written on the cover, and showed it to him.

"Yes," he said. "I want you to read it all. Someone wrote it for me. It is about me, and I want you to come back and tell me what you think. Can you do that for your Poppy, *Chérie*?"

I told him I would.

I opened the little red journal in my room. The inscription on the first page read "To my dear friend, I dedicate the following: Let me wish you beauty, joy, and peace, victories that will every-day increase. Love, Bella."

WHEN I WAS LITTLE, UP TO MY PRETEENS, POPPY'S ASSISTANT AND primary model, Bella, had traveled with him to out-of-town events and spent hours with him at his design studio. She was a tall beauty with long, silky auburn hair, porcelain skin, and high cheekbones. Poppy had choreographed a dance for her on the catwalk to Ravel's *Boléro*, a fifteen-minute orchestral piece that began at a torpid pace, marching drums thumping, and rose in tempo and volume to an ecstatic climax. Bella would end each fashion show with the *Boléro* dance, wearing Poppy's famous "M" dress that could be worn a hundred ways.

With no embellishments, the slinky knit jersey dress looked elegant but safe, with its long sleeves and modest hemline hitting at the knee. On Bella, the dress appeared dangerous. She'd slither onto the catwalk in impossibly high heels, without a bra, hips swaying to the music, her arms in the sleeves of the dress and her hair in a neat bun. When she reached the end of the catwalk, the song would increase in volume and momentum, and she'd peel her arms from the sleeves and pull the neck of the dress over her head.

The audience gasped. It had seemed as if Bella was removing the dress, but instead she'd writhe her shoulders through the neck of the dress and tie the arms around her waist. This was one of the hundred ways. She'd swivel back down the catwalk, loosening her bun, her long, dark hair cascading over her back. As the drums thumped and everyone's pulse ignited, Bella would swirl in time with the music, changing the design of the dress over and over until she spun at the end of the catwalk, hair roping around her neck and covering her face, eyes closed, in rapture at the end of the song.

I'd stare up at her with envy. I could never do this dance. She was possessed, illuminated by a single spotlight, all eyes on her, everyone either wanting her or wanting to be her. Even at a young age, I knew there was something sexual to this dance, to this song, and it both excited and troubled me.

I enjoyed visiting Bella's home. She had a large pool with a diving board and a citrus grove in back of her house in Miami's horse country. She'd let me pick fruit, and I'd mill among the trees, alone in the shade, daydreaming, peeling oranges and eating them whole, sour juice pouring off my chin onto my shirt.

One day, when I was eleven, Poppy picked me up from summer day camp at the YMCA. He was red-faced, his lips drawn tightly into his mouth like they did when he was angry, and he grasped the steering wheel with white knuckles.

"Bella is marrying an eighteen-year-old boy," he said to me through his teeth. "Can you believe that?"

Eighteen sounded old to me, and I didn't have a clue how old Bella was. She could have been twenty-five or a hundred.

"She is ridiculous," he said. "She believes her own press. Never, ever, believe your own press. Do you know what that means, *Chérie*?"

I didn't understand what all the fury was about. I told him I didn't know what that meant.

"When we go places to show my fashions, they bring her roses, they tell her how beautiful she is, they write about her in the newspapers. But I made her. I created her, and she forgets that."

I stared silently through the windshield as we drove.

"And now she is going to marry an eighteen-year-old boy." He hit the steering wheel with the heel of his hand. "She will fail, but I can never take her back."

He wiped his eyes. "I do not want you to see your Poppy like this," he said, his tone changing.

I didn't see what the big deal was, but Poppy was upset. His anger and sadness dominoed onto me, and I started to cry.

"No, *Chérie*, do not cry." He patted my frizzy hair with one hand as he drove. "These are adult problems, not yours."

Then he took me for ice cream at Swensen's. I stood in front of the cold ice cream display with Poppy's hand on my shoulder, both of us walking slowly down the row of colorful flavors.

Once we decided, Poppy opened his wallet and asked the lady loading our cones with mint chocolate chip, "Do you want to see a picture of my pride and joy?" She nodded, and he showed her the wallet-size photograph of the furniture wax and the dish soap.

After she laughed, he turned to the recent wallet-size school portrait of me and said, "That is my little girl."

We licked our cones and I soon forgot about Bella and her impending marriage.

I turned the page of the red journal. Bella's handwriting was neat, cursive, and light, as if she hadn't pressed hard with the pen, or perhaps the ink had faded with time. The entire journal was filled with love poems, florid and clichéd verse about how she felt warm and womanly and on fire with Poppy. I read the next one, then the next.

Beneath green boughs
To lie awake
Rolling gently love to make
Beneath your back
Joining has become
An act sublime
And you are me
I am you

Oh tell me darling
Is this beauty true?

There were poems about Poppy's hands on her body: some explicit, some rambling and repetitive. I read halfway through the journal and couldn't continue. Why had he shown this to me? Did he understand what he was doing, or had the tumor affected his judgment? How had he saved this from the hurricane? What tall shelf had it been hiding on for all these years?

Folded between the pages of the book, there was a fourteen-page apology letter in the same handwriting on purple paper in blue ink:

> *My dearest beloved friend, it's nine o'clock Sunday night. The house is still and in this time I reflect on a day in which I loved poorly and with a mean spirit. You are more lovable than dreams I dreamed and so I have opened myself wide to you. It is very painful, for I burn with the nastiness and impetuosity of my twenty-five years to give and give madly, to fly and sail and soar. My personal spirit has gyrated to a compulsion in movement, grand scope. I shall endure with you until the drops become canyons and we are free without the confines of your world.*

I put the book down and walked toward the bathroom. I wanted to take a long, hot shower, and scrub myself raw with a hard loofah. Poppy saw me as I passed his room.

"Did you read the book, *Chérie?*" he called out.

"I did," I said, backing up and standing in his doorway.

"What did you think of it?"

I didn't like it. I didn't want to know that he had had transgressions. Poppy was my angel who could do no wrong.

"It's beautiful," I said.

"You keep it. I want you to know how people felt about your Poppy."

I stepped into the room and sat down beside him. He looked up at me with wet, cloudy eyes and reached for my hand.

"You are my BaaBaa," he said.

I squeezed his soft hand. I wouldn't hold Bella against him. That was long ago. In my room, I fished a pair of scissors from a drawer and cut off a small piece of BaaBaa, now threadbare after a couple decades of security blanketing. I walked back into Poppy's room and pressed the raggedy square of blue fabric into his hand. He looked at it, turned it over in his hand a few times, and brought it to his face.

"This is the perfect gift," he said.

WHEN I WAS YOUNG, POPPY ALWAYS HAD A RHODE ISLAND RED chicken named Kiki, and it took me a long time to realize that "Kiki" wasn't the same Kiki she had been since I was two. I didn't know what had happened to the other Kikis, but I had the usual suspicions. The Kiki when I was nine, my favorite Kiki, laid the biggest eggs we'd ever seen, twice the size of our other hens.

One summer day, Poppy placed my favorite Kiki in my arms and asked me to follow him to the concrete slab in the shade at the far end of the yard. The chicken clucked as I rubbed my face on her neck. She was as gentle as a kitten, her orange feathers the softest material I'd ever touched, creamier than satin.

"Watch this, *Chérie*. I will show you something amazing." He took a piece of chalk from his pocket and drew a thick, straight white line on the concrete, about a foot long. He took Kiki from my hands and placed her in front of the line.

"You want to learn how to hypnotize a chicken?"

He gently pressed Kiki's head to the concrete, lining her beak up with the line he had drawn. Kiki's head ricocheted off the cement. He pressed her head down a second time, and again she resisted. On the third try, Kiki's head stayed glued to the concrete, her beak aligned with the chalk stripe.

"When she sees the line, she thinks her beak is heavy," he said, "and she cannot move."

Kiki seemed helpless and I pitied her. I had thought of her as a creature similar to me, no more, no less; but there she stood, beguiled by a chalk line. It may have been the first time I distinguished any real difference between our animals and myself. I felt uncomfortable watching Kiki exposed; I didn't like being complicit in her humiliation, thinking she'd stay there forever, doomed to the misfire in her chicken brain that said she couldn't walk away.

Poppy waved his hand in front of Kiki's eyes and she clucked her way into the shrubs, her pointed orange chicken butt sluicing the green waters of our lawn. I ran my bare foot over the chalk line, blurring it into the concrete. Poppy and I fed Kiki and the other chickens leftover spaghetti, then sat in the screened patio watching our pigeons return to roost for the night. I didn't hypnotize Kiki again, but I did think of her differently from that day forward, the way something mythic diminishes the moment it becomes real.

Chapter 15

THE DAY OF POPPY'S BIOPSY, WE ALL WOKE UP BEFORE DAWN AND drove him to the hospital. There were two ring-necked doves in the yard that morning, a male and female.

Nurses prepped Poppy, and the neurosurgeon reassured us that he would be OK. He leaned over Poppy's face and said, "Soli, we're going to fix you up. Don't worry, we're going to get you through this."

I kissed Poppy good-bye as an orderly wheeled him toward the operating suite. We ate breakfast in the hospital cafeteria. Three hours later an orderly wheeled Poppy out of surgery and into recovery.

Poppy closed his eyes and grasped my dad's hand. His head was bandaged like a Civil War soldier's, with a spot of bright red blood in the place where they had opened his skull. It shocked me that the biopsy was this intrusive. He might as well have had the entire tumor removed. I stood over him and stroked his cheek.

"Monsieur Moustaki, how you feeling?" my dad asked.

WHEN I WAS TWENTY-THREE, AFTER THE HURRICANE, AND WHEN my parents and Poppy and I were living in Fort Lauderdale, Poppy and I traversed the Las Olas Boulevard bridge to the beach every week to feed the pigeons and seagulls at the edge of the ocean. Parking was easy there, and the beach side of the road was for pedestrians, not for fancy hotels that blocked the public's view, as was the case on most South Florida beaches.

Poppy held my hand as we crossed State Road A1A toward the beach, the sand in front of us tattooed with spiky coconut palm shadows, like the print on a pair of board shorts. We might have looked like a scandalous item to passersby, a tan trophy girl in short-shorts and a baseball cap with a blonde fountain of ponytail cascading out the back, and a silver-haired man in white linen pants, a white button-down shirt, and a floppy white sun hat covering his ears and driving a shadow over his Greek face. I was a little hungover, as usual, but Poppy didn't know. I lagged behind him and he tightened his hand around mine. I held a plastic sack of stale bread in my other hand.

Down the beach I heard the slow rumble of an ATV, and I squinted to watch it dragging a grader over the sand, leveling millions of mini-dunes forged by the feet of tourists, moms and toddlers, and people who worked night shifts. At the shoreline it churned the seaweed under, making the terrain flat and artificial, but pretty, like a fresh snowfall. I had the urge to run behind it, my line of footprints the only human mark for miles.

Poppy had a favorite seat, a worn wrought iron bench facing the Atlantic. Bathers avoided the boxy shadows cast by low buildings blocking out the western sun; they floated on plastic rafts in the last of the sunlight before the lifeguards would lock away their surfboards and close their stands for the evening.

The pigeons crowded our feet the moment we sat. The seagulls noticed and hovered like noisy kites on strings, able to fix themselves in the air. There were black-hooded Laughing Gulls cawing and swooping, their red-lined beaks open and ready, and bold Herring Gulls, gray and white with red smudges on the bottom of their yellow mandibles, joined by a scavenge of Royal Terns with their pointed blonde beaks and tufts of black feathers like toupees on the backs of their heads.

I opened the sack of bread and placed it between us. Poppy reached into the bag and ground a stale dinner roll between his hands, scattering half of it on the ground and tossing the other half into the sky in front of us. I did the same. Gulls overhead careened into one another's airspace, banking off one another's bodies in a game of hungry, violent tag. Birds flew at us from every direction, from the sea in front and the city behind, the flock growing from dozens into hundreds.

"*Chérie*, have I told you about the pigeons in Paris?" Poppy said, tossing more bread to the pigeons, though the gulls commanded both ground and sky like feathered despots, taking more than their share of crumbs.

"I don't think so," I said, though he had told me stories about pigeons in Paris as many times as there *were* pigeons in Paris. I tossed bread into the air one piece at a time, aiming for a particular Laughing Gull with each toss. He was quieter than the others, and I had a feeling he was hungrier, too.

"When your daddy and your Nona and I lived in Paris, there were ten thousand pigeons for every person. You cannot imagine how many pigeons. The facade of the Louvre museum was alive, gray with moving shapes, every crack filled with feathers, and when they flew, flocks of pigeons covered the sun like storm clouds." He tossed more bread to the pigeons at our ankles, the underdogs in this ravenous scrim. I held some bread crust between my fingers, trying to lure them near, but they were too cautious.

"The buildings were being destroyed, beautiful artworks covered in pigeon poo poo." Poppy talked with his hands, pantomiming statues of Greek mythological characters and antique building faces drenched in pigeon poop. "People in Paris did not like the pigeons, and the government had an idea how to get rid of them."

"They didn't kill them, right?" I said. This was our ritual. He told stories; I pretended it was my first time hearing them.

"They put sedatives into pigeon food. Imagine the whole of Paris covered in sleeping pigeons. You could not walk down the street. People from the government picked up all of the pigeons and put them into trucks and drove them many hours away and released them into a forest."

"That was nice of them," I said.

"Guess what happened." Poppy turned to me, ready for the punch line.

"They all came back?" I couldn't help blurting it out.

"Yes, they all came back!" Poppy laughed and slapped his thighs.

The pigeons in front of us widened their circle at his gesture, but nothing deterred the gulls. They were so close I could feel the breath from their wings on my face.

"The government should have asked me about the plan. Pigeons always come home. Everyone who loves birds knows that."

We fed the birds in silence as Poppy led both of us in a deep breathing exercise. Breathe in. Hold. Breathe out. He said the ocean air cured many ills. The breeze smelled like a tropical cocktail, coconut-ish and limey, with a lick of salt. I closed my eyes and breathed in time to the ocean's waves, despite the cacophony of birds swirling around my head.

When I opened my eyes, Poppy was standing a few feet in front of me, his arms raised like the underwater statue of Jesus, *Christ of the Abyss*, sunk in twenty-five feet of water at John Pennekamp Coral Reef State Park in the Florida Keys, where I had snorkeled a few months before. He held a dinner roll in each hand, the gulls swooping and diving to snatch them. A pigeon landed on Poppy's head, then another on his shoulder. Soon, he was covered in pigeons, all scratching their way to his hands to feed. Poppy's white clothes glowed in the afternoon light, and I sat in awe for a moment before arming myself with two handfuls of bread, intending to join him.

The punctuated *woop-woop* of a police siren startled me. A blue and white police car pulled up behind us. Poppy dropped his hands and the pigeons scattered. A chubby cop stepped out of the car and approached. I thought he was going to ask if we'd seen a criminal, or maybe ask directions, though that seemed unlikely.

"Are you feeding the birds?" he said. I squeezed my handfuls of bread, hiding it in my palms.

"Is it a problem?" Poppy said.

"You're not allowed to feed birds here," the cop said. His cheeks were red and his hairline glistered with sweat. I couldn't see his eyes behind his dark glasses.

"I did not see a sign posted," Poppy said. "We are innocent, just me and my granddaughter feeding a few pigeons for fun."

"Whether you saw a sign or not, it's illegal to feed birds here." The cop mopped his forehead with the back of his hand.

"We have come here many times and no one told us," Poppy said. I nodded in solidarity and smiled big at the cop, but he didn't smile back.

"Please come here, sir," the cop ordered.

The cop directed Poppy to step toward the police car. I nudged the bag of bread onto the ground, kicking it under the bench, and followed them.

"I need your ID, sir," the cop said, reaching into his car and removing a yellow paper pad.

Poppy patted his pants and shirt pockets. "My wallet is in the car."

"We promise not to do it again," I said, my words quick and sharp.

"Sir, can you please step into the car." The cop opened the back door where criminals sit on their way to jail. I grabbed Poppy's hand.

"Miss, I need you to sit on the bench," the cop said, pointing to our pigeon feeding spot.

"I'm going with Poppy."

"Miss, sit on the bench, now."

"Chérie, do as he says." Poppy looked scared, this man I loved who had never been in trouble a day in his life, a guiltless feeder of pigeons.

"Where are you taking him?"

"I'm issuing him a citation and it's air-conditioned in the car," the cop said. Sweat traveled from his sideburns onto his chin. "I'm not taking him anywhere."

I sat backward on the bench on my knees and watched Poppy slide into the car. The cop closed Poppy into the backseat, and then sat behind the steering wheel. They spoke, back and forth, and the cop seemed to be writing, though I couldn't see his hands. My knees dug into the spaces between the bench's iron bars and started to ache, but I didn't move. The pigeons had dispersed, but a few gulls still charged the air around my face, and I waved them away.

Poppy and the cop chatted back and forth like mimes behind glass, and someone must have said something funny, because they both laughed. Poppy gestured as he spoke, and then pointed at me. The cop peered at me through the window, then turned around to look at Poppy. They laughed again. The cop opened his door, stepped out, and set Poppy free.

I ran to Poppy and threw my arms around his middle. He wrapped an arm around my shoulder and squeezed twice, which I took as code for "be calm."

"*Chérie*, this is Officer Hernandez. He grew up not far from where we lived in South Miami."

I shook the cop's hand. It was sweaty.

"Your grandfather is very nice," Officer Hernandez said. "I'm going to forget the citation today, but don't feed the birds here anymore. It's not my rules."

We thanked him. He sat back down in his car with a groan and cranked his air conditioner, then shut the door.

"What did he say to you?" I said as we walked toward the bench to retrieve our sack of bread.

"That bloody sycamore. He asked me for your phone number."

"Really? What did you say?"

"I told him you were fifteen."

I laughed. I picked up the bag of bread and Poppy grasped my hand. We crossed A1A behind the cop's car and I saw him bending over inside, studying something below the dashboard, and in one swift motion I upended the sack of bread onto the trunk of his squad car.

Gulls engulfed the car in seconds, screaming and fighting, swooping at his trunk in a crusade to assuage their appetites, but it looked more like a battle of freedom versus authority, feathers deposing the established order. Poppy pulled me forward by the hand toward the safety of the sidewalk on the other side, and I looked back and waved at the cop, who waved back, then checked his rearview mirror and scowled. Gulls scrambled and tumbled on the car's roof and trunk, screeching and laughing in high-pitched cackles. Poppy looked back at the cop.

"What did you do, *Chérie?*"

"He said not to feed the birds on the beach, but he didn't say anything about his car." I tried to remove my hand from his, but he squeezed harder.

"You have always had a sense of justice, even as a child." He released my hand, then took it again as we crossed the street to the parking lot.

We drove home, toward our own birds, and Poppy told me yet again about the bird market of Paris, slowly, like someone picking up pieces of a memory one by one.

THE SURGEON WALKED IN.

"I have some news," he said. He looked at my dad and shook his head. "Do you want me to say it here?"

"Yes," my dad said. My instinct was to have the surgeon tell us the news in the hallway.

The doctor leaned over Poppy's face. "Mr. Moustaki, can you hear me?" he asked in a too-loud voice, as if he were talking to a child or someone who didn't speak English. Poppy nodded and his eyes opened a little.

"Mr. Moustaki, you have a stage four tumor called a glioblastoma," the surgeon said. "We can't do surgery or the laser knife on this kind of tumor. Do you understand?"

"Is it fatal?" Poppy said in a soft, creaky voice.

"One second," the surgeon said, gesturing for us to join him outside the room.

"This is fatal, I'm sorry," he said to us in the hall in a hushed tone. "I don't know if you want to tell him."

My dad and I started crying. I hated the surgeon. I wanted to smash his face and watch blood spray all over his white jacket.

"How long does he have?" my dad asked.

"It's hard to say. Three to nine months is my best guess."

"Thank you," my dad said, and shook the man's hand. Why was my dad thanking this man? I wasn't going to shake his hand or thank him. I wouldn't even look him in the eye. He was supposed to be our savior.

"There's nothing you can do?" my dad asked him.

"If you want, I'll order a round of radiation, and that might slow the growth. Think about it and we'll discuss options."

We both walked back into the room wiping our eyes.

"Tell me the truth," Poppy said.

Poppy had taught me that where there's life, there's hope—and he was alive. Dr. Z had prognosticated that Bonk had three months to live, and it had been a year since then. Doctors don't know everything.

"It's fatal," my dad said, wiping his face with the collar of his shirt.

Poppy cried, weakly, and I started crying again.

I pulled my dad by his sleeve into the hallway. "Why did you tell him?" I stamped my foot, furious.

"He has a right to know."

Poppy and I believed in magic. In our world, anything was possible. But magic is fragile; it has to be nourished and handled gently, like an egg. The words that should never be said had been spoken, and had broken the magic with syllables and breath: *The tumor is fatal.*

WE TOOK POPPY FOR RADIATION TREATMENTS, BUT THEY MADE HIM sicker. His flowing silver locks fell out in a clump at the radiation site where they zapped him, and I collected some of his hair and put it between the pages of my favorite book, T. S. Eliot's *Collected Poems*, at "The Love Song of J. Alfred Prufrock."

> *There will be time, there will be time*
> *To prepare a face to meet the faces that you meet;*
> *There will be time to murder and create,*
> *And time for all the works and days of hands*
> *That lift and drop a question on your plate.*

When the radiation ended and there were no other choices, my mom arranged for hospice care. The hospice nurse, Terry, arrived at nine in the evening on the first night. She was well over six feet tall, with broad shoulders and frizzy black hair. She wore white nurse pants and a pink scrub top stretched over large silicon breasts. She had a strange, throaty voice with a thick Texas lilt. She had been guiding people into the eternal beyond for years, helping their families cope. Her laughter echoed through the house, and you couldn't help but laugh with her. She was a cheerleader for the dying.

On the second day, Terry arrived before dinner, earlier than expected, and brought us a barbecue feast. This endeared her to my dad, and we all felt that Poppy was in capable, generous hands. Rather than talking to my parents about Poppy, I confided in her, asking about his condition and what we could do. She told me that dying people see differently. They breathe differently. They make peace with themselves and their loved ones, silently, little by little. She was medicating him, she said, so he wasn't in pain. He still communicated with us with hand gestures and mumbling, but essentially we all sat around, watching and waiting.

"This isn't an easy job, helping the dying," she said to me one day when we were alone together, folding laundry.

"I imagine it's not," I said.

"People don't want to live when they get like this."

I folded a pair of my dad's khaki shorts.

"That's what extra morphine is for," she said. "It ends things peacefully."

I excused myself and sat by Poppy's bedside and held his hand as the angel of death folded our towels in the other room. Poppy was sleeping sweetly, the sleep of the healthy, but I knew he wasn't. I walked upstairs and sat in the darkest corner of my closet and drank until my own sleep came hard, like someone smothering me with a blanket.

I had to leave for NYU in the morning. I called my boss, another graduate student, to explain the situation, and asked if I could return late.

"If you're not back Monday, we'll give your room to someone else—someone who wants to be here."

"My grandfather is dying," I repeated.

"Decide what you want," she said. "There are a lot of people who would love to have your job and your room."

"Can someone else take my hours and I'll take theirs when I get back?"

"If you don't want this job, call me back and let me know," she said, and hung up.

This girl had the key to my room and the ability to write me up. She could have me tossed out of the dorm and, with nowhere else to live, tossed out of school. I took her word as gospel.

The next day, I set down my suitcase, approached the hospital bed, and took Poppy's hand. "I have to go now, Poppy," I whispered into his ear. I wanted a moment alone with Poppy, but everyone stood around the bed, waiting for something to happen, and I didn't feel comfortable asking them to leave.

He squeezed my hand. "Please stay," he said, wheezing asthmatically.

"I can't. I love you, Poppy."

"Stay with me," he said. "I need you."

I hadn't realized how much he still understood and could articulate. My parents and the hospice nurse lingered nearby, watching, listening. I needed to catch my train, but once I stepped outside the house, I knew I'd never see Poppy again. I felt heartbroken and numb at the same time, wanting to find a zipper in my skin so I could step out of this human body.

"I love you," I said again. "Do you have anything you want to tell me? I'll write it down."

"Yes, please," he said.

I ran upstairs two steps at a time to gather paper and a pen. I leaned my ear to his mouth, my pen poised over a sheet of lined yellow legal paper.

"Be a good girl," he whispered. I wrote it down.

"Beware the hunters," he continued. I wrote that down, too.

"Always hope," he said.

I tried to stop crying by holding my breath. Poppy paused for a long time.

"Anything else, Poppy?" He was silent, breathing hard.

"Poppy, I'll be a good girl. You don't have to worry. I'll beware of the hunters. I won't lose hope." My chest hitched and my throat ached.

I wanted to leave. I had to leave. If I watched Poppy fall away into oblivion, I'd go with him. What was my world without Poppy? The hospital bed, the hospice nurse, everyone on death-watch—it was too much. I couldn't do it.

"I love you, Poppy."

My mom ushered me away from the bed, and Poppy's hand slid out of mine.

Chapter 16

I WAS HEADING DOWN THIRD AVENUE TOWARD MY DORM, A SACK OF Chinese takeout in my hand, when one of my combat boots hit the dirty pavement then sank into marshmallow, the sidewalk pliable under my shoe. Looking down, I expected to see my foot immersed in wet cement, but it wasn't. I picked up my other leg to move forward and watched my knee rise toward me, then fade downward, but the pavement still felt like syrup. Euphoria climbed my body in a wave and reached the top of my head, which tingled under my hat.

I knew Poppy had died.

I sprang toward the dorm and into the back office to check my mail, passing my boss sitting inside one of the offices with her colleague.

"Hey, there," I trilled, waving as I passed. I still couldn't feel my legs and my head felt as if it were going to float off my neck like a balloon. I hadn't greeted them like that before and they laughed as I passed.

My voice mail had two messages, both from my mom. I dialed her number.

"Your grandfather passed away about fifteen minutes ago," she said, talking low, as if avoiding an avalanche.

"We were all around him, holding his hand. He took a last breath and passed on. It was peaceful. I'll call you back when we make arrangements."

The city murmured outside my window—sirens, a lady screaming, dogs yapping. I opened the window and regarded the pavement. All this noise, these lives proceeding and maneuvering around Poppy's death like a bicycle around a pothole.

I headed to St. Mark's Ale House, where the bartender poured heavy, ordered a vodka martini, dirty, three olives, downed it in two gulps and ordered another before my lips dried. It was noon. I ordered a third martini, and halfway through the drink a dark body floated to the surface and broke the crust of my denial, a reflection so true, so definite and merciless that I felt a sharp pain in my chest: *Was it possible that I was responsible for Poppy's death?* Were we like a bonded pair of birds who languished when the other disappeared? I drained my drink and ordered another.

On my way back to the dorm I detoured into a liquor store for a gallon jug of port wine. In my room, I listened to a message from my mom telling me to buy an Amtrak ticket to come home for Poppy's funeral. *Jump out the window,* the voice said. *You killed the birds and you killed Poppy. Jump out the window.*

The voice pushed through the martinis like a weed through the sidewalk, pushing me toward the ledge. *Jump out the window,* the voice said.

I didn't want to know what the world was like without Poppy. I opened the window. Cold air slapped my face.

Jump, the voice said. *Jump out the window.*

I leaned out. Tiny people milled on the sidewalk below. How would my body look there, sprawled akimbo, a puddle of blood from my head trailing over the sidewalk's lip and into the gutter?

A girl would scream and cover her eyes and her boyfriend would pull her into his chest and hold her. People would stand around me, shaking their heads.

I didn't understand death. To me, when someone died, it was the same as if they had decided to take a long vacation on a tropical island where there was no phone and no way to contact anyone, but they were fine. Maybe better than fine. Weren't they like birds with the cage door open?

I closed the window and staggered to the bed, opened the port wine and drank from the bottle, pondering a way to ask my boss if I could return home for Poppy's funeral. I steeled myself, slapping my cheeks so I wouldn't sound intoxicated, and called her.

"You'll have to see if someone will switch hours with you," she said.

I left a message with each of the other nineteen RAs in the dorm to see if someone would swap on-call hours with me, then poured port wine into a glass and slithered into bed with my clothes on. I stared at the ceiling. My Poppy was dead.

Jump out the window.

I pulled the covers over my head and wept. I didn't want to jump out the window, but maybe I wouldn't have a choice.

I awoke still in my clothes, the glass of port wine in my hand, a red, sticky stain on my pillowcase and in my hair. My phone had no messages. The funeral was in two days. I called the other RAs again.

"I'm leaving another message because no one got back to me. My grandfather died and I have to get back for the funeral. Please, please, please, will someone switch hours with me? It's important. I can't miss it."

I poured myself a glass of port wine and a bowl of cereal.

Jump out the window. Jump out the window. Jump out the window.

An hour later, my boss called. "Some of the RAs called to complain that you're leaving messages trying to make them feel sorry for you. You need to stop. If no one wants to switch hours with you, there's nothing I can do," she said. "Maybe you should take some time off. Reconsider what you want in life."

"I'm in the middle of a semester. I need this job to graduate. I came back, even when my grandfather was sick."

"Maybe this isn't the right time for you to be in school."

"All I'm asking is to go to my grandfather's funeral."

"If you miss your hours you're out of a job and out of your room. We have your key and I can have your things put out on the street. You have a free ride with this job, and you're not going to have it for long."

"I've taken out a lot of student loans to be here. I'm not on a free ride."

"I'm going to have to say *no*," she said. I thought I could hear a sadistic glee in her voice, like a schoolyard bully tearing up a weaker kid's homework.

I called my mom and told her I couldn't come home. I thought she would argue or protest, but she didn't. Years later, I realized that I should have sent my urgent request to someone further up on the university payroll instead of imploring people who were one tick above me in the residence hall food chain, working there for room and board like me. But I was afraid. Not only afraid to rock the proverbial boat and lose what I'd built, but also afraid to go to the funeral.

Poppy never wanted me to be sad and told me many times that I should avoid funerals when I could. I'd hated Nona's funeral, but I'd had Poppy there to hold me. I pictured myself standing in the hot grass next to Nona's cemetery plot where Poppy was to be buried, watching everyone I loved cry and toss dirt onto a coffin. I pictured myself jumping into the hole with Poppy, begging them to shovel the dirt over me, too.

My mom asked me to write a eulogy for Poppy. I sat at my tiny wooden dorm room desk with a pen and jabbed myself in the leg with the pen's felt tip until I created hundreds of little round marks, as if I had a terrible pox. I played connect the dots with the pen marks until my leg had vines and flowers and birds all over it.

I opened a blank journal and recalled Bella's diary dedicated to Poppy, the florid admissions of love for a married man. She didn't know Poppy like I did. How could she? We had the truest kind of love, grandparent to child, no obstacles. I wrote about what Poppy meant to me, compared him to our birds, and used images of him flying. I drank port wine and called my mom and read the eulogy to her. In a few places she said it made him sound like Jesus or some kind of saint. I agreed to tone it down, but didn't agree that my sentiments were misguided.

A FEW DAYS AFTER THE FUNERAL, MY MOM SAID THAT SHE AND MY dad had discussed my going to therapy so I could talk about Poppy's death. I wasn't reacting like someone in mourning, they said. I wasn't reacting at all.

The NYU health clinic gave students counseling services once a week for free, so I called for an appointment. I felt neutral about therapy, not knowing much about it. I wouldn't tell anyone the truth about everything I thought and felt. I didn't want anyone to think I was crazy, after all.

My counselor was a neat, square-shaped woman in her fifties, with long brown hair streaked with silver. She wore chunky turquoise jewelry. I thought we'd jump in talking about Poppy, but instead she wanted to ask me dozens of questions as an evaluation—standard practice for a first session and NYU's policy, she explained. I took a deep breath, ready for the interview. She asked me about my background and my family life, my time at school, and other benign questions. Then she asked me about my drinking.

"Do you drink alcohol?"

"Yes."

"How many drinks a week do you have?"

I asked her what she considered to be "a drink."

She asked me what *I* considered to be "a drink."

I said that one drink was contained in one glass.

"Does the size of the glass matter?"

"No," I said.

"A drink in a shot glass and a drink in a fishbowl would both constitute one drink?"

I imagined what a drink in a fishbowl would be like and smiled. I told her yes.

She said one drink was either twelve ounces of beer, a regular glass of wine, or one ounce of hard liquor.

I closed my eyes and catalogued my weekly drinking. I figured the number at about sixty drinks, accounting for ten to twelve drinks on each weekend day, and about five drinks on each weekday, more or less, but often more. Sixty sounded like a lot, so I cut it in half.

"Thirty," I said.

She fished inside a drawer and handed me a piece of paper.

"Read this and let's discuss your answers."

The paper contained twenty questions. I read each aloud. All of them were about alcohol. When I was done, I stared into her face to see if I had passed or failed.

"If you answered more than three questions with a 'yes,' you're considered an alcoholic," she said. "You answered yes to seventeen of them."

I was here to talk about Poppy, not my drinking, and this lady was shining a light on my messy place.

"Do you feel you drink too much?"

"I drink as much as everyone else. I'm here to talk about my grandfather."

"Most people don't have thirty drinks a week," she said.

"Maybe it's not that many," I said. "How many drinks a week do *you* have?"

"Keep that piece of paper and try to be aware of your drinking," she said. I folded the piece of paper and placed it into my purse. "Do you drink to have fun, or when something is bothering you?"

She was picking at my sensitive spot, and it hurt. "A voice keeps telling me to jump out the window," I said, hoping to send her in another direction.

She straightened in her chair. "A voice?"

"It says *jump out the window, jump out the window, jump out the window*, over and over, and it won't stop."

"Do you *hear* the voice?"

"I don't *hear* it. It's *my* voice, but I can't control it."

"Do you *want* to jump out the window or are you *afraid* that you will?"

"I'm afraid I will."

"You won't jump out the window."

"How do you know?" I said, surprised at her certainty.

"It sounds like an intrusive thought, and people rarely do the things the intrusive thoughts say to do. It's more annoying than real. If the thought told you to kill someone, would you?"

"No," I said.

"You won't jump out the window, either." She glanced at the clock. "We have to stop now, but keep an eye on your drinking and we'll talk about it next week."

I told her I would, knowing I'd never return.

Back in my dorm room, I tacked the piece of paper she gave me onto my bulletin board. It was funny. I was an alcoholic, diagnosed by a real psychologist.

When friends tried to cut me off at the bar or wanted to go home, I'd yell, "I'm an alcoholic! I need more drinks!" I wanted to design an "I'm an alcoholic" T-shirt and wear it to bars.

The psychologist's ideas and her flimsy piece of paper were outdated. Didn't she know that young people drink? Who created this ridiculous questionnaire, anyway? I wasn't about to give up alcohol. I was a *writer*.

I photocopied the paper and carried it with me wherever I went, using it as a kind of drinking game. Everyone I knew in grad school failed the test. No wonder I drank so much. I had a reason—or, rather, an excuse. I could drink as much as I wanted. I was an alcoholic. That explained everything.

Chapter 17

AFTER I'D GRADUATED FROM NYU WITH A MASTER OF ARTS IN poetry, Indiana University accepted me into their creative writing program, where I could earn a Master of Fine Arts in poetry. At Indiana, my teachers and writing workshops made university life gratifying. I loved my students and I wrote copiously. I found a private house to rent in Bloomington so I didn't have to follow dorm rules; I culled my "best friend" birds—Bonk and Sweetie, Little Miss Mango, Jesse, and a few other lovebirds from the flock I'd left with my parents—to live with me.

Still, not even two winters in New York City had prepared this Florida girl for a Midwestern winter. Stuck inside, I longed for a glimpse of the sun. I graded papers, wrote poems, and penned long, handwritten letters to my best friend in Miami, Richard Blanco, who had just won the Agnes Lynch Starrett Prize from the University of Pittsburgh Press for the publication of his first book of poems, *City of a Hundred Fires*. And I drank.

Just prior to moving to Bloomington, I had tossed out the idea that I was a *real* alcoholic based on twenty questions on a piece of paper. I knew what a *real* alcoholic was: someone who drank before five p.m.—which I didn't do. After a few months in Bloomington, I declared two p.m. the proper drinking time, and by the end of my second semester, I downgraded cocktail hour to eleven a.m. You were definitely an alcoholic if you drank before eleven a.m. I never did that.

Until my second year in Bloomington.

Then I abandoned altogether the idea that drinking before a certain time of day designated someone as real alcoholic. I woke up for the classes I taught and fixed myself breakfast: a tall glass of Kahlúa topped with a scoop of vanilla ice cream—for the calcium, of course. My perk-up strategy was called "feed a hangover." I ate two bananas, a can of Chef Boyardee Ravioli, cold and out of the can, and drank some "hair of the dog," alcohol from the night before. The hangover relented most of the time, though I gained thirty pounds in a few months.

As liquor eroded my central nervous system, I became paranoid. I installed hook-and-eye locks on the outside of my closet doors. If the doors were unlocked, that meant a marauder hid inside the closet, waiting to rape and kill me. While blacked-out drunk, I often forgot to replace the hook inside of the eye, and then I'd call my classmates and whisper into the phone that they had to come over and investigate my closet and look under my bed. Eventually, those friends stopped coming over when I called them about the marauders, so I called 911 instead and the cops would show up with their guns unholstered. They'd parade through the house waving their flashlights, shouting at the phantom burglars.

My classmates soon stopped inviting me to parties.

No matter.

I landed a German boyfriend who was in Bloomington on a Fulbright scholarship. He liked birds, and we did our own thing, mostly drinking, drinking, and more drinking. He liked a voluptuous girl, despite him being a lean, muscular boxer. That worked for me as I continued with a diet of burritos, ice cream, beer, and vodka.

And I wrote. If I had one poem due, I wrote eleven. I had little to do but drink and write, which is what my German boyfriend did, too. We held poetry writing competitions in my bedroom, where we'd give each other a first line and twenty minutes to compose a poem. He taught me to concoct German mulled wine, *Glühwein*, traditionally made for the winter holidays, though I made it all the time. He prevented me from drunk driving, even when I became violent, pushing him away from the car and trying to slap his face.

When he was in class, I wrote for hours, hunched over a giant sketchpad, scribbling chained haikus, sonnets, and epic long-form poems, a bottle of wine or cream sherry next to me. I liked drinking alone.

When his visa ran out, my German returned to Berlin. Two weeks later he sent me a six-page breakup letter; he'd found someone else.

Another reason to dive into a magnum bottle of . . . whatever.

One afternoon in the spring of my second year in Indiana, an editor called me from Howell Book House in New York City, a division of the publishing giant Macmillan. My editor at *Bird Talk* had given her my number because she needed a bird book edited. She had liked my work and appreciated that I had turned it in before deadline, so she wanted to interview me for a position editing pet books.

After seven fortifying martinis in the airport bar, I flew from Indianapolis to New York and scored the editorial job. The writing program at Indiana University allowed me to complete my third year from a distance—all I had to do was turn in my thesis, a manuscript of poems. So I moved back to my adopted home, the land of bars and liquor stores open on Sunday, a pedestrian-friendly town where I didn't have to drive drunk.

MY 350-SQUARE-FOOT FIRST-FLOOR TENEMENT APARTMENT IN HELL'S Kitchen was four blocks from my new job at 1616 Broadway, close to Times Square. I had my own office, complete with a window and a view of the marquee for *CATS*, the musical, playing at the Winter Garden Theater. Wasn't it a promising sign that my favorite poet, T. S. Eliot, had written the poems inspiring the play?

My hands shook if I didn't drink a little bit in the morning. I didn't think the tremors were a big deal, and I didn't realize that hangovers were a physical symptom of alcohol abuse. I felt normal hungover.

I liked my boss and my colleagues and edited books on everything from birds to rabbits to grooming poodles. I was a good editor, but soon I was embarking on long liquid lunches. One martini at first, and I'd come back to the office on time. Then two martinis. Then three. After three, I'd close the door to my office and lay my head on the desk and sleep.

The paranoia that began in Bloomington amplified in New York. I scuttled down the sidewalks studying my feet, hurrying to my destination. I felt invisible—not metaphorically; I believed people *actually* couldn't see me, that my physical form had disappeared. I'd aim for people on the sidewalk and if they bumped into me it was proof of my invisibility, proof that I wasn't "crazy."

I had no friends in New York, not even from my NYU days. The only person who chatted with me about non-work-related things was the assistant at work, a comedian/receptionist who didn't want to be there but needed a day job.

Another publishing company, Wiley, the creators of the *For Dummies* series, bought our company, and the other editors quit or were fired. All their projects fell to me, over sixty books at once.

And I drank. I rolled in at eleven in the morning instead of at nine, disheveled and still half-drunk from the night before.

Most afternoons, I crawled under my desk at work and rocked back and forth and cried. Every hour or so, I'd wipe off my face, grab a few file folders, and walk around the office with purpose. Sometimes I'd even photocopy a meaningless document. Then I'd crawl back under the desk and rock some more. Somehow, I still managed to complete my edits.

One day my boss called me into her office, shut the door, and told me that we had a big meeting with the salespeople in an hour. Could I go to the bathroom and try to make myself presentable?

At home, I'd slide under my home desk, next to the trashcan, and rock back and forth, crying. And there I'd talk out loud, saying, "Please God, please God, please God, please God," over and over, asking for something, but not knowing what. We didn't chat often, God and I, but I hoped He hadn't abandoned me, even though I deserved it. The more I drank, the deeper my psyche buried the idea of "alcoholism" within a shiny form of denial I wore like an emblem. Sure, alcoholics drank a lot, like I did, but my problems were way more advanced than any snap diagnosis and –ism word bandied around on sitcoms. I was falling off the edge of the world. Alcohol alone couldn't do that, could it?

I taped tinfoil over my one window and hung heavy dark curtains over it. Light hurt. I'd cry myself to sleep on the hardwood floor most nights, always drunk. I wrote dozens of suicide notes while drunk, reading them in the morning after a blackout, recognizing the handwriting but wondering who'd written them.

After a night of drinking, as the sun rose and people powered to work in their suits, I might be staggering home from a bar. I'd look into their bright faces, coffee cups in their hands, and feel so unlike them, more like an animal sitting in a cave banging two rocks together, begging for help, but all anyone could hear was "clack, clack, clack."

I called in sick most Mondays and Fridays. My boss pulled me aside to show me on the calendar the days I'd missed, and I felt embarrassed—not that the drinking caused me to be absent, but that someone had noticed my pattern.

One early Monday morning, after staggering home from a Sunday night drunk, I tried to let myself into my building and the key didn't work. I grumbled and cursed the lock. The building's super crept up behind me.

"*Estúpida*," he said. I knew the word meant "stupid" in Spanish. I kept trying the lock.

"*Estúpida*," he said again. I glanced at him and willed the key to turn.

"*Estúpida*," he said for a third time.

"*Estúpida* what?" I barked, exasperated. "Did you change the lock?"

"*Estúpida*, you don't live here," he said.

I had been trying to enter into the building next door.

Bonk was approaching twelve years old, and lovebirds aren't supposed to live much longer than that. I didn't feel right about forcing Bonk and Sweetie to ride out another cold winter in New York City, and I couldn't endure having anything I loved that much rely on me when I couldn't even rely on myself. I took the birds back to Florida on a quick trip home, but kept Jesse, the Meyer's parrot. I didn't want to be entirely without a bird, and Jesse was a hardy little guy, my only company, sitting on my shoulder and preening his wings as I drank my Kahlúa milkshake in the mornings.

Chapter 18

ONE HOT AUGUST DAY IN NEW YORK CITY, HUNGOVER, THE HUMIDity clinging to every strand of my hair, I rolled out of bed at two p.m. and headed to the liquor store wearing pajama shorts, an oversized T-shirt, and fuzzy slippers. My complexion resembled the color of the sidewalk, the whites of my eyes a shade of watered-down urine, and the bags under them too big for the stowaway compartment.

I didn't look into the faces of the people on the street. Strangers had become furniture to be stepped around. I envisioned my life as a movie, and I didn't think of other people as having lives—they were actors in the big motion picture of my life, and when those actors walked out of the scene, they ceased to exist. They reappeared when it was time for their lines again.

I stared at my fuzzy slippers as I entered the liquor store on Ninth Avenue. I chose a bottle of Lillet and two bottles of cream sherry. I pushed my money to a disembodied hand; the hand took the money and gave me change. I never said hello or good-bye to anyone behind the counter, in any store, ever. I was too afraid they'd see how sick I was. The hand deposited my bottles into paper bags, placed the paper bags into black plastic bags, and pushed them to me over the counter.

I was more chipper on the way home, bottles in hand, looking up, when a man walked toward me with a Jardine's parrot on his shoulder. This was a rare sight, especially in New York City. Pet stores don't sell Jardine's parrots. You have to go out of your way to find this little African bird with its big beak and scalloped green feathers. I also had a member of the *Poicephalus* genus: Jesse.

The guy almost passed me, but I grabbed the edge of his sleeve. He turned and I said, "I have a parrot like that."

He stopped and smiled. "You do?"

"That's a Jardine's, a *Poicephalus*, an African species. Latin name, *Poicephalus gulielmi*. I have a Meyer's, *Poicephalus meyeri.*"

"No one ever knows what Guthrie is," the man said, impressed.

"You want to come meet Jesse?" I asked the stranger. He could have been a serial killer, but I waged he wasn't. He liked birds.

The man's name was Walden. He was a masseur/songwriter. He admired Jesse and we had a long talk about African avian species. I felt human for the first time in months. Walden lived a block away. We exchanged numbers, and he left.

The next afternoon, someone knocked on my window. I peeled back the tinfoil. Walden had brought his girlfriend to meet Jesse. I was three-quarters into a bottle of cream sherry, which I had been drinking from the bottle for lunch.

"You want a drink?" I said, pouring Walden a glass before he could answer. He waved both of his hands in front of his chest and declined.

"No need to be polite, I have plenty," I said, pushing the glass at him.

"Really, it's fine, I don't want any," he said. He gave his girl-

friend an awkward glance. Had I done something wrong? I tried
to give her the glass, but she wouldn't take it, either, so I drained
it in one draught.

"Can you meet me at the garden tomorrow?" Walden said.
"You can bring Jesse and I'll bring Guthrie." I lived next door to
the Clinton Community Garden on Forty-Eighth Street, a plot
of land about the size of a tenement building's footprint, lushly
planted with seasonal flowers by members of the community,
complete with an apple tree, grape-vined trellis, and beehive.

Of course I would, I told him. I'd made a new friend.

The next day Jesse and I found Walden at the garden sitting
on a picnic blanket, Guthrie on his shoulder. We talked about
birds for a few minutes before he changed the subject.

"Do you always drink like that?" he asked.

"Drink like what?"

"It was the middle of the day and you were drunk."

"Oh, yeah, that. Pretty much." Jesse hopped off my shoulder
into the grass and started treading toward Walden's leg.

"Do you get in trouble when you're drunk?"

"Sometimes."

"Do you miss work because of drinking?"

"Yeah, sometimes." I plucked Jesse off Walden's knee and put
him back onto my shoulder.

"Does drinking affect your relationships?"

"What relationships?"

Walden paused and scratched Guthrie's neck. "Do you drink
every day?"

"Are you psychic?" I asked him. I thought he was reading my
mind. How else would he know these things about me?

"No, I'm an alcoholic," he said, laughing. "There's this place I
go where we talk about alcohol and it's pretty awesome. There's
a lot of nice people and I think you'd like it."

I wanted to say something, but I couldn't find my voice.

"You should come with me. There's a meeting starting in ten minutes right around the corner. It's fun. You'll love it."

"What are you trying to say?"

"You have a problem with alcohol. It's not my place to diagnose you as an alcoholic, but the signs are there."

"You make it sound like a bad thing."

"It can kill you," he said.

"Maybe I'm an alcoholic," I told him. "But I'm not the bad kind." Who was I kidding? Sure, I wasn't the bad kind—I was the worst kind.

Walden stood up and brushed himself off. "I'm going to the meeting now."

"You're taking Guthrie with you?"

"They don't mind. It's a nice bunch of people. You're welcome to come with me, or we can go another time. Call me if you want to talk about these things."

Walden walked away and I shuffled home, feeling exposed. What had just happened?

Walden and I met at the park often with Guthrie and Jesse to give them some sun and chat about his fun alcohol meetings and all the friendly people there. I told him I was happy he had a place to go to talk about his issues. It wasn't for me.

As the months passed, Walden became a bit of a nag, all happy and ebullient about this special anti-alcohol club, trying to lure me there with the promise of coffee and cookies, so I told him I'd stopped drinking. He saw me once through the plate glass window of my corner bar, knocked on the glass, smiled and shook his finger, but he didn't judge.

I had no friends in New York except Walden. Even my closest friend from Miami, Richard Blanco, who had visited me a few months before, told me he couldn't speak to me anymore. Richard had made appointments with people in New York and had included me in his plans, and I had made him late for every meeting, crying because I was too fat and ugly to leave the house, drinking from a bottle of vodka as I stripped to my underwear, over and over, standing ankle-deep in a puddle of wrinkled secondhand pants and dresses, unable to find an outfit I wasn't embarrassed to wear. Once, he left for dinner without me. He needed space, he said, and then he disappeared from my world.

I blacked out nightly, waking to find my towel rack broken; my teapot melted on a hot stove; my cheap coffee table missing a leg; silk flowers plucked of their petals, strewn across the apartment in a tempest of pinks and reds; my hair cut with office scissors into an uneven bob—never knowing how any of it had happened. I drunk-dialed Walden one night to tell him I was naked except for my vomit-soaked socks, and that I was invisible, begging him to make me real again.

The next evening, he sat on my couch and told me he didn't want me calling him in the middle of the night anymore. I wept and told him about the blackouts: waking to find my futon stabbed with kitchen shears, bleeding cotton fluff; finding knives under my pillow and the phone in the toilet; the unanswered drunken prayers to end my misery uttered before passing out on my hardwood floor.

Walden sat quietly for a long time.

"You sure you don't want to go to a meeting with me?" he said. "It can get worse than this, and this is pretty bad."

His meetings would mean the end of my drinking. I needed to drink, and was positive the people in the meetings wouldn't understand what alcohol meant for me: pain management. Physical pain, psychic pain, I had it all, and alcohol usually took it away, though, lately, alcohol had amplified the pain, too, and I needed *more* booze to scrub the widening stain of discomfort and isolation it created. Alcohol had turned on me, pulled a bait-and-switch routine, roped me into a cruel shell game where there was no pea under any of the walnuts.

Walden observed Jesse strutting around on the top of his cage.

"I like Jesse," he said, pointing to the little parrot. "Do you think he and Guthrie could be roommates? They love each other and I'll take good care of him."

"Take him," I said.

"Are you sure? You can have him back any time."

Jesse furiously clanged one of his bell toys, stretched his head toward the ceiling, and whistled. I didn't deserve to have anything around that loved me. I picked Jesse up and kissed him. He stepped dutifully from my hand onto Walden's shoulder.

With Jesse clinging to the back of Walden's shirt, we rolled his metal birdcage from my apartment into the breezeless summer dusk. The wheels rattled over Hell's Kitchen's uneven sidewalks as we passed a couple of high-heeled working girls, who nodded as we struggled the block and a half to Walden's walk-up.

We began the awkward ascent up three flights of stairs, stopping at each landing to breathe and swab sweat from our faces. The wooden tenement stairs had been painted blue many years ago, each step worn and concave in the middle, where millions of footfalls had landed since the nineteenth century.

As Walden keyed into the apartment, Guthrie watched us from a large cage in the corner. He was a gentlemanly bird, quiet, somewhat docile. Jesse had more bite in him: a miniature Napoléon, always placing one zygodactyl foot in front of the other in a deliberate march, searching for books to chew and demanding that someone scratch his head.

Walden placed Jesse onto the play stand on the top of the cage. Jesse perched at the edge and leaned precariously toward me, uttering his typical earsplitting complaint. I turned away.

"He'll be fine here," Walden said.

We stared at each other for a moment, then I stared at the bare wooden floor. Jesse had been a part of my life for over nine years.

"I'll take good care of him," Walden repeated.

I turned and left. My last avian responsibility had rolled down the block into someone else's life. No more birds.

I felt heavy, as if someone had just clipped my wings.

On my way home, I stopped at the corner liquor store for a gold bottle of cream sherry and a bottle of Lillet, and there I was: a girl and her bottles.

I opened the gold bottle, the too-yellow color of little-girl's jewelry, in the cool of the rattling air conditioner, and poured a glass of the amber liquid over ice. It tasted vaguely of cough syrup. I had two. Three. I opened the Lillet and had a glass. I liked it because I had read that Lillet was Truman Capote's favorite drink. I sat on my couch in my underwear and tinkled the ice in the glass, a sound that could put wings on angels.

I felt loose and social, so I decided to foray into the outside world. I did my makeup by rote—it's hard to see with the mirror wavering. For months I had written myself notes on pieces of blank printer paper in Sharpie strokes that read *Do Not Go Out*. I'd tape the note over the crack in the door at eye level, and sometimes the note still hung there in the morning, but other mornings the paper was crumpled on the floor or torn into uneven thirds, and I didn't recall how that had happened. This night, I remembered ripping the note from the door's seam, the crackling tape unsticking itself like a Band-Aid exposing an invisible wound. I crushed the paper into a tight wad, then unlocked the door and exited.

I walked down my crowded Hell's Kitchen street, past prostitutes I recognized, and the gang members with their sweet Boxer dog disguised as a killer in a studded leather harness. I chose a bar on Ninth Avenue and inhaled the pacifying scent of beer, sweat, and cigarettes. The place was crowded, as usual, with skinny girls clad in backless tank tops and jocks wearing Levis and long-sleeved, button-down cotton shirts. I glanced across the bar, recognized someone, and squinted to see her better. The chubby girl stared at me, too, slumped like a frumpy burlap sack of potatoes that had fallen off a truck. She had sad eyes. I squinted harder, trying to remember her face—she looked so familiar—and realized I was staring into a sepia-tinted mirror.

I mounted a barstool, ordered a martini, and tried to bury the last few seconds. The drink couldn't come quickly enough. I ordered another, and ferried it with me toward the back of the bar.

A group of young guys and girls sat around a table in a semi-circle near the fire exit. The group looked safe and professional—all suits and power ties and shiny black shoes.

"Have you seen a tall blonde girl and a shorter guy with glasses?" I asked a guy at the table, leaning into his ear and point-ing into the crowd as I shouted over the jukebox streaming "Kryp-tonite" by 3 Doors Down through speakers on the ceiling. I stood on tiptoes and scanned the smoky room for my imaginary friends.

"I haven't," the guy said, his arm around a pretty brunette, curls hanging over her shoulders.

"My friends aren't here yet. Can I sit with you while I wait?"

The semicircle of bodies skooched and I sat on the end of the booth. We introduced ourselves. I sat with them for another drink and small talk as the songs on the juke cruised from decade to decade, "Disco Inferno" to "Jesse's Girl." After Santana's "Oye Como Va," the guy said, "You don't have friends coming, do you?"

"I do," I insisted. "Maybe they went to another place."

One of the guys at the table brought a round of pink shots on a tray. The drink tasted like liquid Fruity Pebbles cereal.

That's the last memory I have of the night.

I woke the next afternoon in bed, confused, naked, and cov-ered in vomit. Who had vomited on me? I hazily recalled walking down Ninth Avenue with one of the guys from the table, bright lights and snatches of green eyes and a hand around my waist. Maybe *he* had vomited on me. I couldn't have vomited on myself.

I climbed down from my loft to find a yellow screwdriver on the floor next to my stereo, its innards strewn like bullets at a crime scene—circuit boards, metal tubes, and arterial wires—adding to the debris field of broken glass across my living room's hardwood floor.

There had been a struggle. The toilet was filled with toilet paper and overflowing slowly, water half an inch deep on the floor. Who had done that?

The guy from the bar must have brought me home. He came inside and tried to get physical and I resisted, which explained the broken glass and stereo. He raped me, crawled into my loft bed, and vomited on me. Then he cleaned himself off from the rape and clogged my toilet.

Oh, my God. I was a rape victim.

The chain was locked on the inside of my front door. How could he have exited then chained the door from the inside? After the rape and the vomiting, I must have waited until he left and locked the door behind him.

If he had raped me, he likely hadn't used a condom and he probably had AIDS. Now I would contract AIDS.

Still drunk, sweating slicks of alcohol, I dressed myself in jeans and a hoodie and walked to St. Clare's Hospital emergency room. Ninth Avenue was so different in daylight, pigeons and sparrows gathering outside the pet shop, where the employees had tossed old seed onto the sidewalk, and the Italian ice vendor handing a lady a cup of raspberry that would turn her tongue bright blue. On Fifty-Second Street, a few cops stood outside talking to paramedics. I gestured to one of the cops and he approached.

"Something bad happened to me last night," I confided in a whisper. "I was raped."

I wanted to say something else, a phrase he wouldn't have understood: *I have no more birds.* The officer sprang into cop mode and escorted me inside the hospital. I followed him as we bypassed the other people sitting in the emergency room's waiting area. He approached the nurse's station and whispered to them, and he and a nurse led me to a curtained cubby where the nurse instructed me to change into a gown.

The cop and another police officer, along with two nurses, came to take my statement. I told them about the struggle, the items broken in the apartment, and the vomit.

"What did he look like?" one cop asked, pen poised above his pad of paper.

I waited a long time to answer, trying to access memories from the night before. I pictured the guy walking beside me, the lights bright on Ninth Avenue.

"Brown hair?"

"Tell us this story again," said the cop.

I filled in the gaps, telling them about the pink drink, the guys at the table, someone's brother and a girl in a tank top.

"You smell like alcohol," said a nurse. "How much did you drink?"

"I don't know. No more than usual."

A doctor walked into the curtained cubby, followed by another nurse holding a box with capital letters spelling "RAPE KIT" on it. He asked me what had happened and I repeated the story, realizing that if I was the one who put the chain on the door, I might have been the one who destroyed the stereo with a screwdriver and vomited on myself during the night.

The doctor examined me and took swabs away with him to the lab. He told me to wait. I sat there shivering, drunkenness turning into a hangover, still not sure what had happened the night before, but starting to grasp that I had fabricated the story to fill in time that had slipped past me like a ghost.

The doctor returned with the two nurses, one still holding the rape kit.

"You haven't had sex," the doctor said.

I contemplated my bare feet and squelched a dry heave, the stench of bleach sending my stomach into a lurch.

"Do you want to continue with this rape kit?" the doctor asked. "It doesn't seem like anything has happened to you."

One of the nurses huffed. I looked at the box and told them I wanted to leave. The nurse rolled her eyes and walked out of the cubby.

At home, I threw my purse down and called Walden.

"What was up with you last night?" he said.

"What do you mean?"

"You called me all night. You said you were with some guy from a bar and he didn't want to hang out with you, so you freaked out and it sounded like you were breaking things. I told you to sleep it off, but you kept calling, so I took the phone off the hook. I'm sorry, it was late, and I told you not to call me in the middle of the night anymore."

"I don't remember any of that." I slumped on the couch, listening to Walden's breathing, and to Jesse and Guthrie whistling in the background.

"Walden? Can you take me to a meeting?"

Part Three

Chapter 19

WALDEN AND I SAT IN MY THIRD "BEGINNERS" MEETING IN AS MANY days, held in a tiny, stifling church kitchen near Times Square, fans whirring as people filed in. Someone spoke at the front of the room about how he used to drink, how terrible his life had become, and how much better his life was since he had found the meetings. I cried the whole time, head down, and someone passed me a pack of tissues.

Walden nudged me when it came time for newcomers to say their day count. I froze. If I said I was an alcoholic these people would think I *was* an alcoholic, and the proverbial jig would be up. The person at the front pointed in my direction. I had to choose.

I said, "I'm an alcoholic, and I have three days sober." The syllables felt like poison in my mouth . . . but people applauded. I looked at the smiling faces aimed at me. I hadn't done anything to warrant applause.

Walden nudged me again, and leaned into my ear. "I'm proud of you," he whispered.

Proud of me? I couldn't remember the last time I heard those words. I'd heard, "Hey, get off of the table" and "Get out of this bar" and "You're cut off." No one had said they were proud of me in a long time.

Walden and I walked into Times Square after the meeting. I looked into the faces of people on the street as if I were seeing the world for the first time, noticing how the light hit the buildings in the afternoon, smelling car exhaust and the perfume of roasted peanuts from a nearby vendor. I attended a meeting with Walden every day. I lost twenty-five pounds in three months. My hands stopped shaking in the morning. I freelanced enough to quit my job at the publishing house and write full-time, which allowed me to attend recovery meetings day and night, and go to movies and to the all-night diner with other recovering alcoholics in between.

The compassionate people in the meetings taught me that self-esteem comes from esteem-able acts: doing good, helpful acts and learning new skills builds self-esteem, and self-esteem is one of the foundations of sobriety. I accompanied other alcoholics to meetings at detox wards in hospitals, where we told our stories and hoped we reached someone in the dark place where the disease's gnarled roots had grown.

I took drum lessons from a private tutor a few blocks from my apartment, and each time I nailed a Van Halen drum fill, I left feeling good about myself, drumsticks jutting from a back pocket in my tight jeans, earphones on my head, Rush's *2112* album blaring, giving me aspirations.

Walden gave Jesse back. I took Jesse everywhere with me, even into the shower. At my mailbox one day, I opened an envelope to find a greeting card with a panda bear on the front—it was from Richard Blanco in Miami, with these words written inside: "I miss you. I love you. We need to talk. *Besos.*"

The other recovering alcoholics in the meetings talked about God. They said I should have a Higher Power, but that my Higher

Power didn't have to be an old man in the sky or a guy on a cross. I didn't have to believe to stay sober, but they recommended it; they said it was easier to follow the program with a little faith. Some members had difficulty with this, but for me, God felt like a long-lost friend. I thought that sobriety entitled me to the red-phone connection to my Higher Power.

I chatted with God. Did He want me to be sober? Was this my path? Maybe these meetings were only a speed bump, and I could continue drinking once I learned to control it better? I didn't want to quit drinking, but I liked the attention I received in the meetings. It made me feel visible for the first time in years. But drinking was my habit—my companion—and the sober people were trying to take it away.

One hot, summer day early in my sobriety, I decided I wanted a beer, and the compulsion pushed me to the corner deli instead of a recovery meeting. Alcoholism is a complicated disease with a schizophrenic quality. It talks with many voices. For me, it often spoke sweetly, like a kind schoolteacher, telling me it would be OK to have *just one*. Why not? Who was it going to hurt? Was I always going to be the kind of sheep that followed the herd to the shearing station? Or perhaps, on a hot summer day, I could indulge my thirst. No one would know.

I wrapped my hand around the silver handle of the cold beer case. The door's suction relented and I reached my hand toward a cold Rolling Rock. As my fingers curled around the bottle's emerald neck, someone tapped my shoulder.

"What are you doing?"

I turned around, beer in hand. It was Richie, a guy I had met in the meetings who lived on my block. He spoke with a heavy New York accent, had a tattoo on his neck, and looked like he'd kill you if you annoyed him, but he was handsome, with a giant smile and shimmering eyes, and was serious about his sobriety.

"Nothing," I said.

"Why are you holding a beer?"

"Oh, is this a beer? I was here for a soda."

"You're standing in the beer cooler," he said, peeling the bottle from my hand.

"I was going to drink a couple beers," I admitted.

"Well, you're not now." He pointed to the door with his thumb. "Get out of here."

A few weeks later I bounded toward the liquor store, jilted by another newcomer in the meetings who liked another girl instead of me. This time the voice ordered me to have a drink, said it would calm the knocking in my chest and lighten my emotional backpack. *The guy will be shamed that you drank because of his cruelty,* the voice said, and I believed it. I wanted to drink *at* him. As I turned to walk inside, someone tugged my sleeve. Richie.

"Where you going?" he asked.

"Into this liquor store?" I said.

"For what?"

"I was going to drink." I couldn't lie to this guy.

"Well, you aren't now. You're coming with me to a meeting."

"Damn, what are you, my guardian angel?"

"I might be."

Richie blocked me every time I wanted to relapse. I started testing the theory that Richie was my tattooed, motorcycle-driving guardian angel. If I felt close to drinking, Richie appeared. God didn't want me to drink, and Richie was His messenger. Once, I was on a date with a cute guy when Richie walked into the restaurant and both my date and I said hello to him. I was "counting days," unable to date according to the precepts of my recovery program, and my unknowing date had already earned years of sobriety. I had to admit my position as a newcomer to him. My date apologized, paid the bill, and left, leaving me at the table alone. Richie laughed and said not only was he preventing me from drinking, he was keeping me honest, too.

I scraped together six months of sobriety, but it wasn't easy, mostly because I wanted to earn sobriety *my* way, not by listening to the simple suggestions in the meetings. Healing a damaged nervous system takes a long time, and much of that time for me was spent wanting to return to the comfort of my habit. I spoke to God hourly, asking for signs directing me toward every little decision, becoming angry if the signs didn't appear. "Should I have a turkey sandwich?" I'd ask God. If a turkey didn't fall from the sky, I'd wonder why God was ignoring me.

In December 2000, a representative from the National Endowment for the Arts called to say that I had earned a grant in poetry, a prestigious award that came with a $20,000 stipend. I had applied for the grant with a ten-page poem about chickens that I had written in Indiana. I should have been thrilled, but I was uncomfortable. I felt like I didn't deserve the award. I was sure the NEA would call me soon and say they'd made a paperwork error. Or, someone I knew would call and laugh that they had pranked me. I paced my apartment, the fear of the inevitable rising, waiting for the phone to ring. I needed a drink to tamp down the dragonflies in my stomach—and maybe to celebrate. *Go ahead*, the voice said, *you deserve something stronger than a milkshake.*

If I could duck Richie, I could drink. I didn't want to ditch recovery; I just needed a break. It wasn't about the NEA grant. I hadn't been practicing the principles of the recovery program; hadn't cracked the blue book they gave me, which contained all the information I needed to stay sober; hadn't asked anyone to be my sponsor, the person who would guide me through the rough terrain of early sobriety. In short, I did what people in the program called "half measures," which, according to what I heard in meetings, would avail me of nothing—not half of something—*nothing.* Sobriety was supposed to be a miracle, but in this program, if I couldn't commit to the steps I needed for recovery, sobriety would just be a pretty concept, an interesting topic to discuss over drinks.

I told God that if He didn't want me to drink, He could put Richie in my way. Before heading to the liquor store, I sat in a meeting and raised my hand and told everyone about my plan, giving God a chance to stop me, since we'd had that chat. Richie wasn't there. A guy turned to me and said, "Hey, if you want to drink, go drink. We'll refund your misery anytime you want."

If he had said, "Hey, don't drink, it's not worth it, you're better than that, go to another meeting," I may have considered that a sign. Instead, I had received consent.

I prayed again, concentrating on beaming the words into the sky. "God, if You don't want me to drink, send me *another* sign." I shuffled to the liquor store and waited for Richie. I stood in front of the store's window for a few minutes, looking at my reflection in the glass, the huge display bottles calling me inside. I purchased a bottle of Malibu rum and hustled home in case Richie saw me. I placed the bottle on the counter and sat on the couch and stared at it, giving God one more shot at stopping me. Maybe He needed more time. I'd wait for Ritchie to materialize, and continue if he didn't.

I turned on the TV and *The Simpsons* appeared: the episode where the town drunk, Barney, goes to recovery meetings with Homer's help and sobers up. He celebrates his sobriety by taking helicopter-flying lessons. I came into the episode near the end, but I'd seen it before: Barney is flying a helicopter to save Bart and Lisa from a forest fire. Barney and Homer land the helicopter near a Duff Beer truck, which has spilled a six-pack into the road. Barney wants to drink the beer, but Homer won't let him.

"I won't let you give up now!" Homer yells, as he guzzles the entire six-pack so that there's none left for Barney.

"You brave man, you took six silver bullets for me!" Barney says.

I reached for the remote and clicked off the TV.

Nothing but the hum of my table fan. Jesse didn't even flick a wing. I sat there for a few moments before walking to the counter and cracking the bottle of Malibu. It hissed open, and the smell of coconuts displaced the stale air of my apartment. I breathed in the beach, rainbow umbrellas, and suntan oil, Poppy smacking a little ball toward me with his old wooden paddle, ankle-deep in the clear water of the Atlantic.

The blackout wasn't extraordinary. I woke up wearing only socks, shivering, lying on the floor under my loft bed's ladder, vomit in my hair.

The phone rang. It was Walden.

"Get up, we're going to a meeting," he said. He sounded way too energetic for so early in the morning. I looked at the clock. It was past three p.m.

"Who is this?" I croaked, blinking in the half light.

"You drunk-dialed me in the middle of the night, along with most of everyone else we know," he said. "If you don't want this program you don't have to do it, but drinking isn't working for you."

"I asked God to show me a sign if He didn't want me to drink, and He didn't, so I drank," I lied.

"God isn't Santa Claus," Walden said. "You can't give Him orders and lists of things you want and expect them to appear. That's not how prayer works. Get dressed."

Chapter 20

I SAT AT MY TINY DESK AND HELD THE $20,000 NEA CHECK TO THE light when it arrived in early 2001, making sure it was real. The artistic project to go with my National Endowment for the Arts grant came to me as quickly as birds bolt from thunder: Go to Paris. Find the bird market. Buy a caged bird and release it at dusk over the skyline of Paris in memory of the hurricane birds and Poppy. Become redeemed. Write about it all: every feather, every wing stroke caressing the marigold sky, every blink of every eye following the bird soaring over the chimneys and out of sight.

The people in the recovery meetings said it was too soon in my sobriety for an overseas trip alone, with just a few months clean, but I became obsessed with the idea of *redemption*. Maybe finding the bird market and freeing a bird was the grand gesture that could liberate me from the grief and remorse that I believed fueled my drinking. I arranged for lodging in Paris through a travel exchange website. A French girl would stay in my apartment while I stayed in her parents' bed-and-breakfast for the first month; I would spend the second month in her new apartment in the center of Paris. Walden agreed to take Jesse while I was away.

My seat, over the airplane wing, was next to a woman wearing an expensive floppy straw hat with a polka-dotted scarf tied around it, a sheer polka-dotted camisole in the same shade of chocolate brown as her scarf, and pricey taupe designer mules. I perceived her as an Upper East Side socialite type because her clothing was so well coordinated—my outfits were always off-beat, ill-fitting, and peculiar because most of my clothes were from the Salvation Army. Her immense straw purse filled my seat, and she asked me not to sit there. I told her the airplane was full and she grunted, asking me to put her bag in the overhead compartment.

The other people settled into the aircraft, stowing away their bags, plopping their butts into the cramped airline seats. I played with the little screen installed on the seat in front of me, but it didn't work. I fumphered through my bag for the bottle of Valium my doctor had prescribed when I complained about airplane anxiety. I wasn't afraid of flying so much as I was afraid of pilot error, explosions, and engine failure. I'd never flown in adulthood without having guzzled significant quantities of alcohol.

"My friend is supposed to be on this plane," the socialite said. "But I didn't see her in line."

I wiped my forehead.

"I don't know what I'm going to do if she's not on the plane because I'm staying with her family in Paris and I don't have the phone number." She had a nasally, high-pitched voice, like a cat being squeezed. I opened the childproof cap and dry-swallowed one of the little blue pills.

A cute young guy in his late teens sat next to me in the aisle seat. *These are the people I'm going to die with. Maybe the young guy will hold my hand as we plunge into oblivion.*

Panic billowed in my stomach toward my throat, which began to close as we trundled down the runway. My head scorched and my skin turned from clammy to sweaty. *Stop it,* I told myself.

Don't you dare cry. You're going to make a fool of yourself. My eyes betrayed me, tears rolling from behind my dark glasses.

It was bargaining time.

God, I prayed, *if You get me there safely, I'll never drink again. I mean it this time. Never, ever, ever.*

I held my face in my hands as the engines wailed. We caught air. Choking and sobbing, I realized I should have taken the Valium much sooner. I should have had a few martinis.

The socialite asked me what was wrong. After two minutes of sputtering, I told her about my fear of flying. The plane jockeyed in the air, my butt lifted from my seat one moment and pushed into it the next. The screen on the seat back in front of me flickered and a map appeared showing the plane's trajectory to France. There was too much ocean from runway to runway. I ate another Valium.

I sobbed into my hands, snot running into my palms. I didn't want my last six minutes to be spent like this. I wanted to go down with some dignity. The socialite dug through her purse, produced a disc player, and plugged one earphone into my right ear. "This will calm you," she said.

The music sounded like whales crying, blended with a modulated, analog synthesizer. I found myself able to search for a tissue and eat another Valium. A steward told the socialite to turn off her music.

She dug in her purse again and offered a deck of Tarot cards. She shuffled them and told me to cut the deck, and she pulled out a card.

"We're going to land safely," she said. "Don't worry." I looked at the card. It was the *death* card, a gangly skeleton in the card's center, a scythe in its bony hand. A flush of panic accelerated into my chest and face.

"That's a good card, it's not what you think. It means *change*, not death. I'm telling you, we're fine." She shuffled again and asked the deck out loud if her friend was on the plane. The deck said no. She did this several more times. "I don't know what I'm going to do when I get there," she said.

I asked her, through choking sobs, if she would do a reading for me. It could distract me, and give me some indication about landing safely in Paris.

"OK," she said, shuffling the cards, "but I'll have to charge you five dollars."

I fixed my eyes on the seat back in front of me and continued to sob, the kind of crying where hiccups and hyperventilation complicate the deep breathing and sighing that real crying requires. I grabbed the vomit bag from the webbed hammock where they keep the evacuation directions and hyperventilated into it. The bag made a sound like someone dancing on a piece of corrugated fiberglass.

The guy next to me asked what was wrong. Wrong? How could he tell something was wrong?

I removed the bag from my mouth long enough to tell him I was afraid of flying.

"I shouldn't tell you this," he said, and paused, "but my mom died in a plane crash."

I removed the bag from my mouth again. "Commercial jet?" I hoped he would say she'd died in a two-seater and had been flying the plane herself, while intoxicated and having an epileptic seizure.

"Yeah," he said. "It was a big crash. A lot of people died."

I managed to tell him I was sorry. "How old were you?"

"Four. You learn to live with it, you know?"

No, I didn't know. What was wrong with him that he'd travel by plane knowing firsthand how unsafe they were?

"Did she say she'd charge you five dollars for a Tarot reading?" he whispered. I nodded. He rolled his eyes.

The socialite, convinced by the Tarot deck that her friend wasn't on the plane, turned her attentions back to me.

"Do you mind if I do some healing on you?" she asked. I shook my head and breathed into the vomit bag. She closed her eyes and waved her hands over me like a child would over a top hat during a magic trick.

"I can feel your pain," she said. "It's coming from up here." She placed her palm on my head and told me she was taking the pain away. Five hours and fifty minutes to go. I swallowed a fourth Valium.

The steward asked if we needed anything. The socialite requested a glass of wine from his cart and handed it to me. The wine plunged hard into my gut. I asked him for another. As I held the plastic cup, watching the surface of the blood-colored liquid ripple in time with the engines' whirr, I felt a fuzzy sheen of apprehension starting in my toes and rising through my scalp, spreading like mint in an untended field.

I had done it again. I'd taken a drink. Hadn't I *just* prayed that if we arrived without incident I'd *never* drink again? I felt something else crawl up my spine, into my neck—a rubbery, numbing layer of peace so thick a kid could bounce on it at a birthday party.

I guessed we landed, because the socialite was wheeling me in a luggage cart through Charles de Gaulle Airport, toward the luggage carousel. Everything was fuzzy, covered in white auras from the skylights overhead.

"We're here?" I croaked.

"Give me your luggage tags," she said. I couldn't move. She grabbed my purse and sifted through it.

After collecting my two heavy bags, she wheeled me to the taxi stand. The socialite gave a slip of paper she had found in my wallet to the driver and told him to take me there. She helped me out of the luggage cart and dumped me headfirst into the backseat.

"Have a good trip," she said, slamming the door as the taxi pulled out of the airport.

Chapter 21

THEN THERE WAS THE GREAT MILKY SKY OVER PARIS. THE HEAVENS looked new, extraordinary, and I imagined I understood it as a bird might. I had arrived at the airport unbroken, a shattered fox-hole prayer still welded to my tongue.

Slumped in the taxi's backseat, I tried to appreciate something of the French highway, which reminded me of the hideous strip of State Road 441 near my parents' home in Fort Lauderdale. But we were driving *away* from Paris, not into it. The giant arch at La Défense, on the outskirts of Paris, faded in the distance. My home for the month of July—an English-style town house in Saint-Germain-en-Laye, was outside Paris. It had never occurred to me to look up Saint-Germain-en-Laye on a map. I had assumed it was a part of Paris, the way the East Village is part of New York City, but it was more like Queens—an upscale, French version of Queens.

I dumped my bags in the steamy, infinitesimal, slanted attic room and sat on the narrow, springy bed. The room was decorated with fashion magazine ads and American movie posters, Corona and Budweiser bottles, a few stuffed animals, and the various knickknacks a seventeen-year-old girl would possess: three porcelain Dalmatians, an array of miniature perfume bottles, shot glasses, and a yellow candle in the shape of a duck sitting in a basket.

The neighborhood was pretty, blossoming with pink and orange roses and rhododendron. The family was welcoming: the businessman father, Piers, solid, well put together, and handsome in his own way; the mother, Gilbertine, a pleasant-looking, tidy woman with a nurse's smile and short blonde hair, a stay-at-home mom with three kids; Marie, twenty-three, living in my apartment in New York while I was in Paris; Corinne, seventeen, a lovely girl in her last year of high school; and Arnaud, fourteen, a gawky but well-mannered junior high school kid.

Their eldest daughter had misrepresented our apartment exchange situation. She said her parents ran a bed-and-breakfast and I would have the entire top floor to myself, with a separate entrance to my part of the house, and I could come and go as I pleased. But after instructing me on how to use the front door key, Gilbertine told me I couldn't leave or return after they had activated their burglar alarm for the evening.

Not only was the house not a bed-and-breakfast, there wasn't even a lock on my door. I had a bathroom, also without a lock, and the door wouldn't stay closed. No shower curtain, but there was a large mirror in which anyone walking into the bedroom would see me in the shower in all my naked glory, trying to keep water from puddling all over the floor.

The house was so *quiet*, a black-hole kind of quiet, the world suspended like a pond carp under a crust of ice. I felt betrayed, and my paranoia jangled to life. Maybe this was a trap. Maybe these people were part of the sex trafficking trade and would sell me to a sleazy girl-biz entrepreneur and I'd end up locked in a cage in a faraway country, forced to perform acts beyond my imagination. Maybe they were serial killers. Maybe this was just going to be a boring, restrictive month with strangers, not the freeing, redemptive journey I had imagined. Or, the serial killer thing.

I listed my options: Leave this place and return to New York City, where ambulances, shattering glass, and the sound of prostitutes negotiating rates outside my window lulled me to sleep every night; take the train to Paris, find a hotel, and charge it to my credit card; or kill myself—a decidedly better fate than being sold to sex trade traffickers.

I walked down the thin, winding stairway of the home and, at the bottom step, through choking tears, told the family I must leave.

"You are tired," Gilbertine said. I nodded. "Come, eat something with us."

The four of them made space for me at the table. Piers poured me half a glass of red wine and placed salmon on my plate, then offered me part of a baguette. The wine tasted like guilt, but I told them it was delicious, staring at the wine in my glass as if I'd never seen this type of liquid before. I couldn't look at their faces as I ate, and then slithered back upstairs, telling them I needed to rest.

I called my mom and whispered into the phone, explaining about the lies, and how I was trapped with dangerous strangers. I felt wilted and irrational and wide awake, like a balloon hanging in a small, swirling draft.

"Go to sleep," she said. "You're not thinking clearly."

I cupped my hand around my mouth and rasped into the phone. "I believe I'm in danger here."

"Put someone else on the phone."

I called for Gilbertine to pick up the extension, and listened for snatches of their conversation.

"Is this typical of her behavior?" Gilbertine said.

After a few minutes, she hung up and climbed the creaky stairs to my attic room.

"It would be a good idea if you could get some sleep," she said. "You'll feel better after."

All I could do was nod. She shut the door behind her, the door that would not lock.

I didn't want to spend my NEA money on hotels—that's not what it was for. I slipped under the green gingham comforter, still wearing jeans. The bed groaned like a badly constructed ship, and when my knee hit the thin wall it rattled the photo of the three suntanned siblings standing in front of a plateau in Monument National Park, according to the caption on the frame.

After half an hour of sweaty sleeplessness, I minced downstairs for a drink of water. The family stared at me like a strange animal they pitied because it seemed disoriented. I began to weep.

"I need to leave," I said. "This isn't what I thought it would be." I had come to Paris to find the bird market and free my soul of its burdens, perhaps having adventures to write about along the way, which seemed improbable in the suburb of Saint-Germain-en-Laye.

"Your daughter told me this was a bed-and-breakfast." They looked confused.

"You knew you were coming here and then you would have our other apartment in Paris by yourself in August in one month," Gilbertine said.

"You can't go back to New York," Piers said. "You made a deal. Our daughter is working there."

I wanted to tell them that their daughter scammed me; but Gilbertine had a kind face and sympathetic eyes, and looked so maternal and comforting. I decided to trust fate. Maybe living with a family would soften my splintered New York City nerves.

Around midnight, I crawled into bed under the lowest slant in the attic, pulled the covers to my chin, and closed my eyes. It was so quiet the family could probably hear me clear my throat.

There was rustling in the small, walled garden behind the house, the sound that marauders make before they shoot rappelling ropes through the window, climb up, and rape and murder everyone in the house. I tiptoed to the window and searched for the source of the sound, but saw only blackness.

I had two choices: either let the marauders enter the house and kill us, or wake the family and hope they could drive the marauders away. I tapped on the parents' bedroom door. Nothing. I knocked louder. Gilbertine opened the door wearing a white cotton robe, looking exhausted.

"There's someone in the garden," I whispered. "Behind the house." I pointed in that direction. She said something in French to her husband and he walked past me as we followed him downstairs. He found a flashlight in the kitchen and beamed a current of light through the sliding glass door into the darkness.

"There's nothing here," he said.

"I swear I heard something," I urged.

He opened the door and stepped out into the night. Gilbertine and I waited behind him. After a minute he called for us to come outside. He stood under my window, pointing the flashlight into a bouquet of crispy fallen leaves and onto a huge prickly hedgehog rummaging in the underbrush.

"There's your intruder," he said. It was cool to find a hedgehog in the middle of the night. I hadn't realized they ran loose in France, like squirrels. I slunk back to bed. My first impression on these people had been solidified: I was a fragile, weepy, irrational, paranoid nut job.

Chapter 22

THERE'S NO WAY TO DESCRIBE PARIS AS A WHOLE. HEMINGWAY SAID Paris was "a moveable feast." That's as right a description as any. What happened to me was this: I walked. I turned a corner. I saw the most beautiful object, street, or piece of art I'd ever seen. I took a deep, soul-scrubbing breath and resumed walking. I turned another corner. I saw the most extra-beautiful object, avenue, or sculpture I'd ever seen. Then another corner. Another pinnacle of most beautiful object, alleyway, or building. The corners of Paris didn't end.

Gilbertine put Corinne in charge of showing me how to find Paris. Corinne walked me through the twists and turns of her neighborhood to the bus stop. We hopped the bus to the RER train station and rode the train to the Charles de Gaulle–Étoile station and emerged from the tunnel directly across the street from the Arc de Triomphe. It was the most beautiful manmade object I'd ever seen: a giant red, white, and blue flag waving beneath its arch, tiny people walking around on top, cars whipping around the traffic circle, forming their own lanes. Poppy had stood here. I could feel him.

Block after block, Poppy's assertions were true. Maybe he even undersold the city's magnificence. The sidewalks on the grand boulevards—such as the Avenue des Champs-Élysées—*were* as wide as rivers, sidewalks like liquid waterways gleaming with a mineral intensity in the sun, flecks of silver, blue, and gold winking from the granite under my sandals. Corinne walked me through the Tuileries Garden in front of the Louvre. It was the most beautiful park I'd ever seen. The Parisians put museum-quality art outside for pigeons to perch on, like Rodin's sculpture, *The Kiss*, two naked lovers entwining forever in bronze patina, ignorant of us watching them and of the pigeons on their heads, the male lover's hand on her hip, the female lover's arm scalloped around his neck—they would never be lonely—or without birds.

Corinne and I took a table at Vendôme, an outdoor bar over-looking the Louvre and the gardens. I knew I should find a recovery meeting in Paris, but didn't know where they were, and like a garden-variety alcoholic in a relapse, I let that minor detail deter me.

"Should we order a drink?" I asked her.

"Alcohol?"

"Yes," I said, nodding. "A drink."

She paused. "It is not typical to have a drink in the daytime."

This was why I didn't want to nest with a family. I didn't like living under a microscope, all my shameful secrets on a slide for everyone to see.

"But maybe a glass of wine," she suggested.

I had forgotten that the French don't consider wine "drinking."

"We should share, no?" she asked.

I agreed, reluctantly, that sharing would be fine. We ordered cabernet, which came in a roomy glass that looked a quarter full. We took turns taking small sips.

"Do you have a boyfriend?" Corinne asked me. I didn't want to say that I hadn't had a real boyfriend in years, but since I had

gone on a few dates with another newcomer from the meetings
before I left, I told her about him, that he was a waiter and lived
near Times Square.

She swept her long bangs from her eyes. "I have a boyfriend,
too," she said. "We went to bed one time, but my parents don't
know."

I finished the wine in a gulp. "Just the one time?"

"I wanted to wait until eighteen, but he wanted to do it. Don't
tell my parents, OK?" She pulled a cigarette from her purse and
lit it. I wasn't sure if she knew how lovely she was, so unlike most
American teenagers, so possessed of herself. Most French teen
girls looked like this—shiny hair, lean bodies, flawless skin, pouty
mouths, and tiny waists underneath perfect bust lines and finished off with long legs and perky backsides. I was still over-
weight, and the alcohol didn't do any favors for my complexion.

"You shouldn't smoke," I said. "It gives you wrinkles."

"Eh, *oui*?" she said, wrinkling her brow. "I do not think so."
She took a long drag from the cigarette.

"Should we order another glass?" I needed more wine. Once a
little alcohol entered my system, my body begged for more.

She pouted her bottom lip and looked at the ceiling. "It is
early, no?"

Instead of ordering more wine, the teenager dragged me to
her favorite department stores, which were having summer sales.
She took me to the apartment where I'd spend August to see the
renovations on the small one-bedroom—there would be new
floors and fresh paint on the walls. I longed to be staying there.
On the way back to the suburbs, Corinne kept silent as I tried
to find the way to her house on my own through the winding
streets. I couldn't, and she had to intervene.

This family was charming and pleasant, but I was still sullen.
If they were on the phone, they apologized. If they had an errand
outside the house, they apologized. If they ran out of orange

juice, they apologized. Gilbertine left breakfast and lunch out for me every day, invited me to dine with them most nights, and even did my laundry, folding my undies and handing them to me in a wicker basket. I couldn't appreciate any of it. Poppy would have charmed Gilbertine's family as if they were a flock of birds.

The next day, it rained. I didn't want to walk around Paris in the dampness, so I stayed in my attic room and listened to drops patter on the windowsill and read T. S. Eliot poems, trying to memorize the words to "The Love Song of J. Alfred Prufrock," which I believed to be the most perfect poem written in the English language. I had a lock of Poppy's hair in a small plastic bag and used it as a bookmark.

The next day, Sunday, I'd find the bird market.

GILBERTINE TOLD ME THE BIRD MARKET WAS NEAR NOTRE DAME cathedral. I had a map, and the cathedral was on it, but the bird market wasn't. I walked down the Champs-Élysées, through the Tuileries Garden, and turned toward the Seine. I stopped a guy selling newspapers and asked him where the Marché aux Oiseaux was located. He pointed down the street and indicated I should turn right somewhere, but I walked away unsure of his directions. In all the times Poppy had told me about the bird market, I never asked him *exactly* where it was located.

Walking along the river, I found myself on the Quai de la Mégisserie, a street running parallel to the Seine, shops on one side, the river on the other—and Notre Dame in plain sight, with its twin towers and exposed rib cage of buttresses. Then—birdsong. Outside a store called Animalerie, a large cage held an enormous red chicken, along with several white doves and a duck. Next to it was a cage crammed with white doves, and another with budgies of all colors. I took my time watching the birds and cooing to them. I didn't want to rush.

Inside that first dark, crowded store, filled with cages of birds, pens of puppies, a pig, some ducks, and a cage filled with kittens, the guy behind the counter wore what looked to me like a butcher's apron, and I couldn't determine whether this was a pet store, the bird market, or a place where locals bought live birds and other animals for dinner.

The next store was the Oisellerie du Pont Neuf. The word *oisellerie* sounded close to *oiseaux*, which means *birds* in French. *Oisellerie du Pont Neuf* was a huge, clean, bright pet store filled with puppies, kittens, fish, chipmunks, turtles, and birds.

Was this the bird market? A collection of pet stores on one street in Paris? I walked down the street along the Seine, past several flower and plant stores, and discovered another pet store with birds in cages out front, similar to the first store, though larger, and this one housed plenty of reptiles, too.

Maybe years had changed the bird market since Poppy had been there. It wasn't anything like he'd described, but I guessed this was it. I returned to the first store, where the pigeons lived in crowded conditions and may have been used for food, and approached the man behind the counter, busy helping someone buy a French Bulldog puppy. The place was raucous with the voices of patrons, birds, and dogs. A rooster called from a back room, and the whole store smelled like a barn—hay and dung and the sweet, funky smell of birds.

"*Pardon,*" I said, waving my hand at him. After a few minutes he acknowledged me and asked me in French what I wanted.

"I'd like to buy a pigeon," I said. "A bird. *Oiseau.*" I pointed to a cage filled with standard, everyday rock pigeons. The man didn't understand, so I gestured for him to follow me and I tapped on the cage and asked him how much for one pigeon. He told me they cost eighty-five francs, about twelve dollars at the time. I said I would take four. They were inexpensive enough. I'd reap four times the redemption.

"Why do you want them?" he said.

I doubted I could explain redemption in a way he'd understand. "I just want them," I said.

He cocked his head and peered at me through the corner of one eye. "What you do with *les oiseaux?*"

"Just to have them," I said, shifting from one foot to the other. I felt nervous. I didn't understand the reasons for his questions. I wanted birds. I was in a pet store. Do the math.

"No," he said.

"What?"

"No, no, no." He waved his hand in front of his face as if to clear away a bad smell.

"I'll take one, then."

"No," he said, pushing past me. He opened a half door and walked behind the counter.

I followed him. "Excuse me, *pardon.*" He waved me away again. I wanted to explain about Poppy, about my mission, about regret and redemption and grief and love and the National Endowment for the Arts, but my French wasn't good enough. Tears stung my eyes and I wiped them away before they breached the rims. I waved and caught his attention again.

"*Quoi?*" He stood with his arms folded across his chest.

I pointed to a few brown adolescent ducks near his feet. If I couldn't buy a pigeon, a duck would do. I could release it in the fountain at the Tuileries.

"Can those swim?"

He laughed hard. "You are going to tie a ribbon to her neck and float her in the Seine like a child's boat?" He rolled his eyes and turned his back on me.

Hot tears rolled down my face. I put on my sunglasses and walked out of the store. The bird market was not what I had expected.

MY DAD HAD TOLD ME THAT A SINGLE WOMAN ISN'T ALLOWED TO SIT at a bar alone in Paris because that means she's a prostitute. I found the closest café and ordered a ham sandwich and two glasses of wine, not caring if I seemed like a "working girl" drinking in the middle of the day.

I replayed the exchange in the pet store. Why wouldn't the man sell me a simple pigeon? What did he think I was going to do with it? Had I become the kind of person to whom someone would not sell animals? Was this my karma? I had killed my bird friends in the hurricane and no more bird friends would come into my life. I ordered more wine.

Five glasses down, on my way toward obliterated, I ordered *moules frites*, mussels and French fries, and a glass of Stella Artois beer. When the mussels came, I asked the waiter for a spoon; he sneered at me and threw a spoon at the table, which bounced and hit me in the chest. I was too drunk to react. I ate my food slowly, ashamed. A guy next to me was drinking something red. I pointed to it and asked the nasty waiter to bring me one.

He arrived with a pear-shaped glass of Kronenbourg 1664 beer and a small, shapely shot glass filled with a sticky red liquid, which after a sip I discovered was grenadine. I supposed I should pour the grenadine into the beer, so I did. The concoction tasted like fermented cough syrup.

I wobbled onto the sidewalk after paying the bill. What to do next? I could drown myself in the Seine. I could jump off the Eiffel Tower. *Walk in front of a bus*, a familiar, disembodied voice said. *Walk in front of a bus.*

As I wandered, bumping into passersby who cursed me in French, I spotted a hair salon. A new hairdo always made me feel better.

No one in the salon spoke English. I flipped through a copy of *Vogue* and chose a pretty model with minky, dark brown hair, and showed the photo to the colorist, who applied dye, and after the requisite wait washed my head and wrapped it in a towel. A few strands of hair wisped from under the towel, and I pulled them out. Orange. An unnatural, unholy orange.

I snatched the towel off my head and turned the pages of *Vogue* again to the model with the brown hair. The colorist apologized and led me back to the sink, where the she reapplied darker dye. Now my hair was purple with red streaks, and the hair closest to the scalp was still orange. I looked like the third ring at Barnum & Bailey.

The receptionist, who spoke a little English, translated for the colorist and told me my hair would be brown after she blow-dried it. My locks took on a lilac sheen once dry, the orange brightened, and the red shimmered when I jiggered my head under the lights.

My bottom lip quivered. *Do not cry*, I told myself.

I wrapped my hands over my face and sobbed. I left the salon after they made me pay for the botched 'do, and walked straight to a clothing store and bought a hat.

I woozily found my bus and rode it to the station closest to the house, but when I stepped off the bus nothing looked familiar. I walked in a direction that looked correct, swaying down the street, stumbling on my own feet, arriving at a sign reading "Versailles." I had been walking out of town toward the highway. The sun disappeared and the sky softened into a hazy gray. Songbirds trilled in the trees overhead, telling one another to roost for the night.

Gilbertine had written succinct directions on how to use a French pay phone on a piece of scrap paper, so I found one near a church and described my surroundings, and five minutes later sat inside her car, weeping.

"What happened to your hair?" she said when we arrived home and I'd stopped hiccupping.

"I told them to dye it *brown*," I sputtered as she handed me a paper towel and a glass of water.

"You should have called me before you went," she said. "That's the color they dye everybody's hair. I had that color not long ago. Wash it and it will come out. Wash it six times."

She was right—the dye ran off my head, onto the shower floor, the prettiest shade of purple.

Gilbertine knocked on the door and told me that my mom was on the phone.

"What's happening over there?" my mom said. "The nice mother asked me if you were always this emotionally unstable. I told her you were prone to emotional outbursts when you're tired. Get some rest, will you?"

I said I would. Instead, I washed my hair again, watching Paris swirl in a lavender cloud down the drain.

I TOLD THE FRENCH FAMILY ABOUT MY EXPERIENCE WITH THE BIRD market—excluding my inability to buy a bird—and discovered I'd missed the bird market by a few blocks and had wound up in the pet shop and plant district instead. I'd have to wait until next Sunday to see the bird market, but that was the day after Bastille Day, the French National Day, a holiday like the Fourth of July, and I figured the market would be closed. Instead, I toured the Louvre and fell into deep, steamy love with a young guy in his early twenties in a painting from the 1500s by Bronzino. He had wise, dark, mature eyes for his young age. I wanted to undo the tight white collar at his neck and kiss the hollow between his clavicles. He had been dead for over four hundred years. I was so lonely and he was so cute, I wanted to cuddle his bones. I thought about what Dr. Z would say if I told her I had found a nice young man—but he lived in a painting in France. "He lives where?" she would exclaim. "He'd better not like birds." I stopped to gaze at my boyfriend in the grand gallery nearly every day, suspended forever in his oils and turpentines, peering at me beyond his Roman nose, eternally young. I bet he did like birds.

I spent my weekdays avoiding alcohol and going to recovery meetings, which I found with a quick dial-up search on my old laptop. I hung out with other recovering alcoholics on vacation, eating a lot of bread and chocolate and going to museums. I decided not to find the bird market until after I moved into Paris proper on the first of August. What if I didn't have the resolve to set my redemption bird free? I couldn't bring a pigeon home to the French family—they might think it was for dinner, or at the very least confirm their suspicions that I was a lunatic.

PIERS LUGGED MY HEAVY BAGS INTO THE ELEVATOR, A CREAKY OLD wood and stained glass box protected by an antiquities act so it couldn't be replaced. The wood and wire interior doors didn't close all the way, so someone had rigged a couple of twist ties that had to be held together or the elevator would stop.

The sixth-floor apartment on the Avenue de Wagram couldn't have had a better address in Paris. I leaned out the window to gaze at the light going soft over the Arc de Triomphe, which I could have hit with a baguette if I threw it hard enough. The Eiffel Tower radiated in the near distance, glowing yellow from the inside, a spotlight turning around its head, a beacon for lost tourists floating through the streets.

I kissed the family good-bye and watched them drive away. I felt certain I'd never see them again. I could have made friends for life. I could have said good-bye with everyone happy, with my dignity and self-worth intact. But.

I was in Paris. It was no time for remorse.

I stripped to my underwear and leaped around the apartment. Every cell of me felt free. The noise from the street was immense: cars whooshing by, alarms wailing, people screaming to one another, the music of the city. I breathed for the first time in a month. This was what I wanted. Lines from my favorite T. S. Eliot poem rose on my lips:

> *There will be time, there will be time*
> *To prepare a face to meet the faces that you meet; . . .*
> *And for a hundred visions and revisions,*
> *Before the taking of a toast and tea.*

Yes, there will be time to prepare a new face. Time to murder the old me: the morose, drunk me. Time to create. Time yet for a hundred visions and revisions. Yes.

I was in Paris, salvation flocking in undulating feathered masses, soaring free over the city, waiting for my redemption to join them.

Chapter 23

SUNDAY MORNING I WALKED ACROSS THE OLDEST STANDING BRIDGE in Paris, the Pont Neuf, to the Île de la Cité, stopping in the middle to watch a *bateau mouche*—a barge-like boat filled with tourists—cruise beneath, entering into shadow and reentering into light. It was the middle of the afternoon under a cloudless sky, the heat making me feel perishable and flimsy, my shirt stuck to my sweaty back. The Seine glittered gold on top of green, each wave a mirror, the blurry reflection of old, magnificent Parisian buildings swaying in the boat's wake.

A wash of nerves rose from my feet and into my stomach. I wanted to turn around. I didn't want to see the bird market. What if it was like the dreadful pet stores? What if Poppy had transformed a minor marketplace into a grand attraction for the sake of a good story?

I walked toward a large cobblestone courtyard surrounded by neat shrubbery that ended with the Place Louis Lepine, a charming open square bordered by the Palais de Justice and a block or so from the Cathédrale de Notre Dame on the bank of the Seine. Policemen stood in clumps, talking, maybe off-duty or on a break.

I approached a chubby cop and he smiled, his wildly crooked teeth gleaming.

"*Pardon*," I said, "Do you know where I can find the bird market? *Marché aux Oiseaux?*"

"Ah, *oui*," he said. I smelled onions on his breath. He pointed back the way I had come. "This street, and turn . . ." He gestured with his hand indicating left. "It is there."

I thanked him and he winked at me, and I felt possessed to kiss him on the cheek, so I did. As I walked away from him, the uneven cobblestones melted under my feet. A ray of golden sunlight drew me around the corner, and I followed it like an ethereal line on a nonexistent map.

Birdsong.

Lovebirds. Cockatiels. I followed the voices of the birds, watching pigeons gliding overhead, their wings whistling through the breeze off the Seine.

The street was one block long, lined on either side with rows and booths and tables. Birdcages hung over the heads of proprietors. Pigeons shuffled in figure eights among giant stacks of millet spray and barrels of loose bird feed—birds so bold they didn't move aside as I walked through them.

The bird market looked like a haphazard swap meet: jumbles of bird supplies piled on top of one another, birds in cages arranged not by size or species, but by where someone found a sliver of space. Bird toys hung on provisional trellises. This was not a grand, organized tourist attraction, but the magic grew as I walked. There were English trumpeter pigeons with feathers on their feet, giant red roosters, fluffy white Japanese silkie chickens with tufted heads, lovebirds in color mutations I had seen only in magazines or heard about in rumors. The street smelled like flowers and the musty perfume of birds, whose voices swelled inside the alleyway and bounced off the breeze.

I was standing at the center of the universe.

For someone who knows birds, the bird market is grander than Napoléon's tomb, more magnificent than the Tuileries, and deeper than the catacombs. I saw what Poppy saw: birds in every possible hue, sunlight burnishing every feather. Rare grass keet species in mutations nonexistent in the United States preened one another in small cages. A rooster howled, and ducklings squatted in the hay in their little pens. A crowd petted a large, friendly orange chicken, and I petted her, too. It had been years since I'd touched a live chicken, and I was eight years old again, standing in Poppy's backyard, holding Kiki, feeling safe and loved.

Poppy had walked here, had breathed this air, heard these sounds, felt the same cobblestones under his soles. I sensed him walking beside me, outside of my peripheral vision. We strolled together, watching birds flit from perch to perch. I turned around to grasp his hand, but saw only strangers behind me.

I walked from vendor to vendor for more than an hour, peering at each cage of birds as if they were van Gogh paintings. One of the bird vendors spoke enthusiastically to his customers, pointing to his pigeons, canaries, and finches gleaming in the afternoon light. He had a kind face and obviously loved birds the way he loved the air in his lungs, without cognition, the way I loved them.

"*Pardon*, do you speak English?" I said, tentatively, pointing at one of his cages. "How much for the pigeons?"

He turned toward me and studied me up and down.

"Where are you from?" he asked in a heavy French accent.

"New York," I said, not understanding what that had to do with the price of pigeons.

"You go back soon?"

"Yes."

"What you do with the pigeon?" He thrust his chin at me with each question, like an unconscious tic.

"I was going to let it go," I said, making a motion with my

hands like wings flying into the sky, staring into the sun, imagining my pigeon rocketing out of sight.

He wiped his hands on his pants. "So, you will buy my pigeon and let it fly and it will make love with other pigeons and come back to me and infect my birds with disease? Is this what you want?"

"That's . . . not . . . what I want at all," I stammered.

"*Eff,*" he said, and waved me off. "No, no, no." He stared into my eyes so hard I flinched and slunk away from his table.

There were plenty of pigeons at the bird market, so I walked to a nearby group of cages, but before I could hail the next vendor, the first vendor yelled to him in French. I couldn't understand everything, but I caught the gist: *Don't sell anything to this American.* I heard laughing, and I had to tell myself the snickering wasn't about me, though it may have been.

I approached another vendor, and saw the second vendor gesturing to him and talking in French, pointing to me, and shaking his head. A cruel game of telephone had begun, and there was no way to stop it. One vendor laughed, called me over, and offered to sell me a fat, scared skunk huddled in a cat carrier.

Was my money not good here? I didn't understand. I stood in the middle of the bird market like a toxic island as people parted to avoid me, careful not to run aground on my shame.

I crept away from the bird market, head down, disgrace dripping from my clothes. Maybe the vendor knew the awful man at the pet store who also refused me a pigeon, and somewhere there was a poster with my photo on it and the directive that I not be allowed to purchase a bird. I wandered with no direction for an hour and found L'Église Saint-Eustache, a Gothic church in front of which stood a sculpture by Henri de Miller, *L'Écoute*, a behemothic, disembodied stone head leaning its cheek to rest on a disembodied stone hand, ear listening to the sky. But the hand and cheek didn't touch. The face and the hand sighed toward each other in a gesture of the next obvious movement that would not arrive. The head would never rest on its palm; the palm would never feel the head's repose.

I sat on a stone bench near the head, angry and distraught. My hands were shaking. I'd come all this way for the bird market, to see what Poppy claimed was a magical place, yet the vendor's rejection seemed predestined. I'd contested fate and lost.

A young boy nearby, maybe twelve years old, crept up on a group of pigeons with his camera. Such a sweet moment, those beautiful birds picking at crumbs in front of a towering cathedral. *That will make a great photo,* I thought, at the exact moment the boy raised the camera over his head and then swung it hard, holding onto the neck strap, using the camera as a club to hammer one of the pigeons with a loud *thwap.*

I ran toward the boy and the stunned pigeon, which was wobbling on the ground in a blur of black feathers and pink feet, deserted by its flock mates.

"I got one!" the boy declared, grinning triumphantly.

I reached to grab the pigeon as the boy dodged my grasp. I'm sure it looked like I was reaching for him. He ran to join his mother, camera dangling from his pigeon-mutilating hand.

The pigeon wobbled away from me and flew off, its tail feathers brushing my fingers as I closed my fist in the air, hoping for a handful of pigeon, but grasping my own palm instead. I sat on the ground, winded and stunned, then brushed myself off and slumped back to my spot on the bench, scanning the ground and the eaves of the church for the camera-struck pigeon, but they all looked the same from a distance.

A group of school-age kids traipsed by, the boys kicking one another's shoes, trying to trip one another. I had an idea. When I was underage, I asked shabby-looking men in front of the 7-Eleven to buy me Boone's Farm wine and let them keep the change. I could use the same tactic and ask a native Parisian to buy me a pigeon. I scanned the park for teenagers. Surely one of them would want to score a few easy francs.

I approached a teenage girl and boy and asked them to help me, but they didn't speak English. This happened a few times. Either the people didn't understand, or they thought I wanted something for free, like money or a ride, and brushed me off. Finally, two older teenage boys semi-understood my Frenglish and rudimentary pantomime.

I pointed to a group of pigeons and enacted flying motions with my hands, then pointed toward the bird market and, in the most childish French, offered them each a hundred francs, about fourteen American bucks apiece, if they'd buy me a pigeon and bring it back to the park.

They nodded, snuffed out their cigarettes, and took one hundred francs for the pigeon as well as fifty francs each for them, with fifty more each when they delivered it. I told them it didn't matter what kind of pigeon they bought, what gender or color. I wanted a standard, everyday pigeon like the ones at our feet, and pointed to the bench where I'd wait for them to return. The boys pocketed the money and kissed me on both cheeks before they strolled out of sight.

I sat on the bench, elated. *In your face, fate. I've got this.* Tourists trolled the stone head, crouching inside the nook between its palm and cheek for photographs. The day cooled and the tree above me whispered and sighed in the breeze.

After thirty minutes I wanted to jog nearby for an orange Fanta and a panini, but couldn't leave my spot in case the boys returned. An hour passed. Then two. The sky softened into periwinkle, then gray, with yellow-streaked clouds like rough brushstrokes on a cheap canvas. My tongue felt big in my mouth.

Three hours. Four. They weren't coming back. I turned around on the bench and cried, hoping no one would see what a fool I'd become. I wiped my face, put on my dark sunglasses, and shuffled toward home. The faces of passersby looked uncaring, solid with indifference. I wanted a drink.

I slumped to the counter of a dark and cool *tabac* and ordered a *café crème* and a chocolate tart. I'd drown myself in desserts rather than alcohol, at least for now—finally taking one suggestion I'd heard in my recovery meetings: eat dessert to quell the craving for a drink. A couple of round old Parisian men stood at the counter to my left. My coffee arrived, thick and sweet. I licked my upper lip.

One of the two old men next to me snorted, the one with no front teeth and several chins, and said to the bartender, in French, "What do we have here?" I understood him.

"American," said the bartender, disinterested, drying coffee cups with a dishtowel.

The man snorted again, elbowed his friend, gestured to me with a nod of his head and a waggle of his chins, and said, *"American, eh? Je préfère coucher un cheval."*

Roughly translated, he would rather go to bed with a horse. I didn't know whether to be further dejected or laugh. I stared into the mirror at the back of the bar, hoping nothing showed on my face. I finished my coffee in two gulps, paid for it, left the chocolate tart, and ran around the corner, making sure to check street signs so I'd never enter that *tabac* again.

I wanted to laugh about being less worthy of intercourse than a mare. I wanted to laugh about the folly of the entire day, the Shakespearean way this pigeon mission was shaking out, me thinking that buying a pigeon was the ticket to a clean conscience—but I couldn't.

Dusk turned to night and the lights of Paris blazed on all at once. Not far from my apartment, a corner restaurant appeared with a red awning and a chalkboard easel in front advertising tonight's special, *moules frites*. Inside, the wooden bar was glazed with warm, inviting yellow light.

I sat on a shabby leather barstool and scanned the bar. The bartender asked what I wanted and I was going to order *moules frites*, but from the depths of my psyche, from nowhere and everywhere all at once, I formed my mouth around the words: *frozen daiquiri*.

I was in Paris, France, not a palm tree in sight, ordering something served with a cocktail umbrella and a slice of pineapple.

Without a wince or hesitation, the bartender turned to his rack of bottles. He filled a stainless steel cocktail shaker with ice, and poured a sickly green-colored liquid into it—sweet and sour mix—and a shot of rum. He moved with the deliberation of an executioner. He spilled the contents of the shaker into a blender. The blades smashed the ice into slush, the green liquid almost phosphorescent, like the fluid inside glow sticks.

I licked my lips. I was inside that blender. I *was* that drink.

He stopped the blender, and in one motion lifted both the drink and me and poured us into a daiquiri glass, with its curvaceous hips, wide rim, and delicate stem. He set the drink in front of me. I tasted it in my mouth before I even touched the glass, felt the cold, icy mess on my lips, sweet, sour, hot with the island taste of sugar cane and lightning over the ocean. It would burn my head, warm my chest, set my feet on fire. Then I'd have another.

The bartender turned around, maybe to ring me up or clean a glass, and I bolted so fast I knocked over my barstool, leaving the drink deserted and the tab unpaid. I ran to the apartment and sprang up the six flights of stairs, two at a time. My hands shook as I locked the deadbolt behind me.

Chapter 24

THE NEXT DAY I STROLLED WITHOUT DIRECTION, STILL REELING
with humiliation from the pigeon debacles and near alcohol
relapse. The heat formed hazy waves of translucent mirage shimmering off the broad sidewalks, urging tourists to tuck into cafés
and drink Perrier *menthe* or smoke under the shade of a *tabac*'s
awning. Sweaty and numb, I walked on autopilot, wondering how
I'd messed up the trip so badly. I didn't feel damned or unlucky—I
felt stupid and impotent. I'd been full of hubris, the quality that
killed all the antiheroes in Shakespeare's tragedies, thinking I'd
waltz into Paris and set myself free as easily as opening a can of
beans. I felt beaten. The bell had been rung and my fight was
over.

I found Les Deux Magots on the Place Saint-Germain-des-
Prés, one of the cafés where the existentialist Sartre and his lover
Simone de Beauvoir had dined and philosophized, and where,
sometimes, Hemingway had strolled over to say hello. I still felt
embarrassed entering restaurants and bars in Paris as a single
woman, overly worried that I'd be mistaken for a prostitute.
Waiters glowered at me like I didn't belong.

I told the maître'd I was waiting for a friend. He placed me in a small, charming garden area in the back of the restaurant. I ordered a ham and butter sandwich and a *café crème* from a cute waiter. The weather turned breezy, lemony sunlight polishing everything it touched.

The waiter brought my sandwich and coffee and asked about my friend. I shrugged and pointed to my wrist, where a watch might have been, but I never wore one.

A brown sparrow lighted on the table to my left, swiveling his head, hopping forward, then back, then forward again, jerking his head all the while as if he had a nervous tic. I pulled off the edge of my sandwich, ground the bread between my fingers, and tossed it to him. Then there were three sparrows, twelve, twenty. I folded my hands in my lap and held my breath as they swarmed my table and my plate, pecking and chirping and multiplying.

I broke off more of my sandwich. It didn't scare them. I ground the bread between my palms and placed my hand on the table. The little birds hopped onto my palm and ate from it. They stuffed themselves on my sandwich as I studied how they moved, tried to tell them apart, and tossed crumbs to the timid ones who kept a distance. I'd been desperate to release a bird, and here were a quarrel of them, coming to *me*.

Four birds sat in each of my hands, the bold males with their dark beaks and black masks, the females with their drab plumage, all trusting me to keep my end of our unspoken bargain—they would honor me with faith and I wouldn't move. If Poppy were here he'd have attracted ten times the sparrows. A hundred times.

In the middle of my reverie, the waiter swooped toward my table and whooshed his arm into my flock, scattering them onto the tops of the umbrellas. He frowned, shook his head, and removed my plate.

———

I DIDN'T LIKE THE IDEA OF WANDERING THROUGH THE RED-LIGHT district by myself, but it was the middle of the day and I hoped my map of the city would distinguish me as a tourist, not a lady of the night—or the afternoon. I wanted to see the Moulin Rouge. After two Métro changes and a one-block walk up Place Blanche in the searing heat, there stood the windmill of the Moulin Rouge. It was smaller than I had imagined. The vanes on the windmill were still; the meager breeze couldn't break the heat enough to evaporate sweat, much less power a windmill.

Below the sign, green plastic netting wrapped around a horizontal pole spanning the width of the windmill. This kind of netting, along with pigeon spikes and plaster owls, was placed all over the city so birds didn't perch or nest where they weren't wanted. As I studied the windmill, something moved in the netting at the far left, at least twenty feet over my head. A pigeon hung there, caught by one foot in the plastic webbing.

I walked closer. It hung downward in a perpetual headlong free fall, wings spread out like an upside-down Jesus. He struggled to free himself, flapping wildly and resting again. He panted in the heat, and if he didn't free himself soon he would die of exhaustion or dehydration.

Passersby bustled around me on the sidewalk. Had I been in New York, I could have found help. But I didn't speak French well enough to start such a conversation with anyone, and I had no idea if Paris even cared enough to have a paid official on "pigeon detail," someone from their animal care and control center, like the one in New York.

"Do you speak English?" I asked an older gentleman who looked American. He shook his head. I stopped a young German couple whom I heard speaking English, but when I pointed to the bird they kept walking.

I walked into the dark and cool Moulin Rouge. On either side of the long, plush red hallway, posters of seminude showgirls in glitzy costumes with grand feathered hats hung as advertise-ments for the show. I approached a young, pretty blonde woman behind a wooden podium and she smiled.

"There's a bird outside with a problem," I said, pointing toward daylight down the dark corridor. "Let me show you."

"Ah, you want to see the show," she said.

"No. There's a bird in trouble. I need help. Come look." I ges-tured for her to follow me. She didn't move.

"I do not understand," she said. "You want a ticket for the show . . . tonight?"

"No, listen," I said, searching for the right words. "Outside, there's a . . . *oiseau mal. Oiseau mal.*" I gestured like a bird flapping its wings and continued pointing outside. She shook her head and squinted at me. All I had managed to say was "bad bird."

I turned away, cursing myself for resisting Nona and Poppy when they tried to teach me to speak French.

The bird was a typical rock dove of the order Columbiformes—a city pigeon—with a two-bar pattern on his wings and white pied markings on his dark face and neck. This one was a big male, his breast shining with iridescent purples and blues, his belly and mantle light gray.

To the left, under the trapped bird, was a dirty white door, which I assumed led to the backstage area of the Moulin Rouge. To the side of the door was an intercom. I knocked on the door. Nothing. I pressed the intercom. Once. Twice. Three times. A crackling voice spoke.

"*Oui?*"

"Can someone come here?" I said. "*Oiseau mal.*"

A male voice punctuated the static, something in French I didn't understand.

"*Oiseau mal!*" I yelled into the intercom.

Nothing. I buzzed the intercom again. *I'm sorry, little one,* I thought, staring at the helpless bird. *I'm trying to save you.*

"*Oiseau mal ici!*" I yelled into the intercom again, remembering the French word for *here*, banging on the door again.

The door cracked open and a dark-haired Frenchman appeared. He looked about twenty-five years old, a little mussed up, kind of sexy. His white T-shirt was dirty, as were his well-worn jeans, but his face was fresh and ruddy, and he had an intense alertness in his dark eyes. He said something in French I didn't understand.

"*Oiseau mal,*" I said, like an idiot, beckoning him to step outside and pointing toward the pigeon. He stepped outside and surveyed the problem.

"Ah!" he said, finger pointing to the pigeon. "I will make the rescue." He walked inside and shut the door.

The bird continued to struggle in the heat. As the minutes passed, a small crowd gathered, murmuring in French. The young man emerged from the door carrying a tall wooden ladder, which he rested on the wall beneath the pigeon. He slipped on work gloves and climbed the ladder to the top. As he reached the pigeon, he pulled a large pair of shears from his back pocket. I bolted to the ladder and rattled it.

"No!" I yelled. "Don't cut his foot off!"

"No, no," the guy said, waving a hand behind him. He turned back to the bird, but I wasn't sure he had understood.

I climbed a few rungs of the ladder while he used the shears to cut the green netting away from the bird's foot. He held the pigeon tenderly with one gloved hand as he removed it from the mesh. I blushed and backed away.

As he descended the ladder, pigeon in his free hand, I saw that the bird's foot was malformed—a clubfoot—which is how it had become caught in the mesh. Its leg was bleeding. A woman with a cart full of groceries pulled up beside me and clicked her tongue.

"Poor bird," she said. "Poor, poor bird."

"You speak English?"

She nodded. "Poor bird," she said again.

I reached my hands out to take the bird from the cute guy as he stepped onto the sidewalk. He gave me a gorgeous, warm smile and handed me the bird. The crowd applauded as we made the hand-off, and dispersed. The guy took the ladder inside.

I had a pigeon.

"What will you do with him?" the lady with the grocery cart asked. She looked to be in her late sixties, dyed red hair sprayed into bouffant perfection, lots of blush, and a black penciled-on mole above her orange-lipsticked mouth.

I turned the bird over in my hands. He was calm and warm, breathing hard, but not struggling. I could have launched him right there, but he was injured. And I needed to process the weight of this sign, this billboard, this cosmic, divine, feathered Jumbotron.

I told the cart lady I didn't know what to do with the bird. Once, in New York City, I had paid $45 to have a pet taxi take a baby pigeon that had fallen from its nest to a bird sanctuary on Long Island. Another time, I took an injured city pigeon I found in Times Square to the veterinarian for $85 worth of X-rays and paid $60 to have it humanely euthanized because it would not have healed.

Here, I was clueless.

"Come," the lady said. "I know a place."

She waved me in her direction as she pushed her cart toward a side street. I followed her around a corner onto a shady, narrow lane. The temperature dropped ten degrees. We wound through the back alleys of Pigalle, her pushing the cart, me holding the pigeon to my chest with both hands. I had no idea where we were going, or if I should be following her in the first place.

The pigeon felt soft in my hands and I wanted to rub him on my face, but resisted. He looked around and blinked. One of his feet was normal, but the other was clenched into a knot, a piece of twine wrapped around it, digging into the flesh. I surmised that his chick-hood nest had been composed of trash and string, and this piece of twine had wound around his foot when he was a squab, and stayed there as his foot grew, causing it to grow abnormally. He didn't seem in pain, though there was dried blood on his foot and feathers.

The cart lady stopped in front of an open window in the middle of a block and rapped on the frame.

"Juliette!" she called in a loud whisper. She pronounced the name like "Juli-ET-ah." "Juliette!" she called again.

We waited a moment in silence, the pigeon resting in my hands, calmly regarding our surroundings. The cart lady turned to me and cupped her hand to one side of her mouth, as if to tell me a secret.

"This is a place of prostitution," she said in a loud whisper, tapping on the window's frame again.

Oh. My. God.

No person in the world besides this lady with her cart knew where I was at that moment. "Juliette!" the grocery cart lady called again.

A woman came to the window—Juliette, I presumed—and the two women exchanged words in French. Juliette opened the door and gestured for us to come inside.

I stepped into the dark, narrow hallway, the grocery cart lady behind me, blocking my way out. I clutched the pigeon tightly as I walked deeper into the brothel, which looked like a regular apartment. The walls were painted a light icy blue. A beige couch sat behind a glass coffee table, and flowers bloomed in a porcelain vase in the corner below a series of three small paintings of birds.

Juliette was in her late forties and had a soft, round face and chestnut hair pulled into a loose bun. She wore a long skirt, sandals, and a flowered peasant top. She walked with determination. I guessed she was the madam, not one of the working girls, but what did I know?

Juliette tried to wrench the bird away from me, but I wouldn't release him. The women exchanged more words in French, which I didn't understand. I had to leave there, bird and all. I felt dizzy. My hands tightened around the pigeon.

Juliette managed to force the bird from my hands and walked him further into the brothel. I followed on her heels. I should have focused on finding my way out rather than on keeping the bird, but I wanted him. I needed him.

I followed her into a tiny clean bathroom. She plugged the sink, ran the water, and dunked the pigeon into the sink a few times, feet first. She dried him with a washcloth and examined him. Aside from the raw, clubbed foot, he had a small wound on his hip. Behind me, the grocery cart lady spoke to Juliette in French, and Juliette answered, then walked out of the bathroom, further down the long, dark hallway, further from the front door, my only way out.

Juliette *kind* of knew what she was doing, I conceded that; but I still wanted my pigeon back. What was she going to do with him?

Juliette approached a door at the end of the dark hallway with me trailing an inch behind her. She opened the door and the brightness of daylight stopped me in the doorway. As my eyes adjusted, a large sunny picture window came into focus, and below it perched various pigeons and doves on wooden dowels and plastic makeshift trees, strutting on the floor and eating seed from large tin baking pans. Juliette was not only running a brothel—she was running a pigeon sanctuary. She had regular rock pigeons and wood pigeons, but she also had white fantail pigeons and a pair of ring-necked doves.

The birds winged around the room, dust clouds glittering in sunbeams as they whipped the air beneath them. They seemed comfortable in their sunny space. Some of them stood in wooden cubbies, like those found in a kindergarten class where kids put their backpacks—but here, the birds nested in them. Juliette released my pigeon into the room and he flew straight to a pan of seed. Another large pigeon pecked at him, and Juliette shooed the bigger bird away and chastised it in French.

All I could do was thank her. *"Merci."*

"Merci," she said back, smiling. Why was she thanking *me*?

I emptied my wallet, all 150 francs, and gave it to Juliette. The lady with the grocery cart gave Juliette fifty francs, too. Juliette thanked us again and kissed me on each cheek.

As we left, I noticed hundreds of pigeons crammed into the crevices of the building and under the eaves around Juliette's apartment, cooing softly. I hadn't seen them before, too focused on the pigeon in my hands. The door shut behind us with a loud click and the pigeons bolted in every direction, a wave of gray bodies launching themselves into the sky as if to cool it with their wings. They were glorious. I felt like flying, too. The pigeons schooled in a wave above the alley, swooping over the rooftops, then careened back toward us in a black, synchronous swarm, and lighted again in the eaves.

The grocery cart woman and I kissed each other good-bye on both cheeks and I strode back into the sunlight onto Boulevard de Clichy. I felt something lift in me, a gate unlock, a fortress crumble. Poppy stood beside me, his silver hair swept behind his ears. I smelled his cologne. I took a step. He took a step. I reached for him. We strolled arm-in-arm along the broad sidewalks, ambling across the Pont Neuf, over the cobblestones on the other side, until birdsong drew us toward the bird market like the beam on a lighthouse.

I followed punctuated staccato trills, melodic whistles, such distinct voices—lovebirds. We rounded the corner into the bird market of Paris, a halo of sunlight hanging over it like a messenger. There was something here I needed to learn, something I could almost touch, out of my reach, like a frightened bird.

"Poppy, please help me release a pigeon for you."

"*Chérie*, release yourself." He pointed to the sky and I followed his finger to a flock of pigeons swirling against the glowing white summit of the Sacré-Cœur. "You are already free."

I released his hand and lifted from the ground, my feathers igniting the air beneath me. I saw him from above, pointing, waving, and I waved back with my gray wings. Then he was with me and we soared over Paris, playing with the last rays of sunlight, the Eiffel Tower an etching against the sky.

A motorcycle backfired. The pigeons at my feet launched into the sky in a symphony of grays and blacks, their wings whisking the air around my head. I waved my hand in front of my face to clear the dust and looked around for Poppy, but he was gone. I turned, trying to spot him among the crowd, but saw only the backs of strangers.

I stood in place for a long time, thinking that if I moved, I might blow away. I felt light, like wings. Poppy was here with me, in a black velvet sports coat with a silk handkerchief in his pocket, his footfalls in cadence with mine, speaking in hushed tones, endowing me with powerful wings, feeding me Paris in small crumbs, and making sure I ate.

I gazed out my window that night and saw all twenty-four of my birthday dove stars, the light from the tips of their wings pecking out a signal in a cosmic Morse code that I understood. I couldn't translate the message into words, because the message didn't come through that way—it spoke to my heart directly, in a feeling I can best describe as *loved*.

We're on the beach at Crandon Park on Key Biscayne, Poppy teaching me to play paddleball with his worn wooden racquets as the sun wends its way west and the moon arrives early, a white ghost against the blue sky: I'm seven and naked from the waist up, the ball a little blue planet soaring between Poppy and me, etching our love indelibly in this space. I'm the best-loved girl on the beach. Poppy and I oblige the ball's orbit regardless of gravity, sending the ball on its favorite path, jumping against our paddles like seconds into creation. My wrist remembers the ball's strike against my paddle, the whole beach brimming with our indiscriminate destiny: his last breath is twenty years away. I can feel it in the ball's perfect arc. I can see it in a handful of sand.

I would rewind those beach days if I could, give myself up to the counterclockwise turn of time. There's a tumor that never starts, his hair blackens, I shrink as the ball turns again, I'm a crumb, then not even an indication, Nona pressed to his starched shirt and velvet jacket, the ball flattening, flying, reviving itself. He's smacking the ball to no one, then there is no ball, no lesson, beach, or memory—just the bird market of Paris, Poppy walking into the birdsong like a sonic fog, shaking the cold off his wings, imagining me, maybe, in a future where he'd have a granddaughter he can teach to charm birds to eat from her hands.

Author's Note

Birds remain an important part of my life, but I don't breed them anymore. There are too many abused, neglected, and homeless birds that need help and homes, and I don't want to contribute to the problem. Some endangered species need to be bred to ensure their survival, and some birds are domesticated, such as canaries, certain pigeons and doves, and society finches; I don't argue against the breeding of those.

I also don't oppose the breeding of most finches, budgies, lovebirds, cockatiels, parrotlets, and some grass keet species—small birds that are easy to care for with a little knowledge and attention. The bigger birds are far more complex, and I believe only people who can provide for *all* their needs should keep them.

There is also a sound argument that breeding birds saves species from poaching in the wild. If domestic breeders make hand-raised birds available, the people who rape the rain forests of feathered creatures won't have a market anymore. Birds are a miracle, and though not everyone is equipped to keep them, those who are able to handle these fussy, feathered supermodels *can* give them happy, healthy lives.

This being said, I feel sad when I see a bird in a cage.

Bonk, my feathered green angel, lived to be sixteen—seven years beyond Dr. Z's diagnosis of inoperable cancer and her prognosis of six months to live. She spent the last few years of her life in a large flight cage at my parents' house in Fort Lauderdale. My mom called me one afternoon to tell me that she thought Bonk was dying. Bonk had faded over a few days, sitting on the bottom of the cage and refusing food, and I knew it was her time. I called Dr. Z and she suggested not rushing Bonk into the office, which would stress her even more. She said to make Bonk comfortable.

Sweetie seemed to understand Bonk's condition and pushed his head underneath her chin when she couldn't hold her head up anymore. I talked to her on the phone and I can only hope she heard me telling her I loved her. She passed away in the middle of the night. Bonk, my faithful, miraculous friend who saw me through the darkest times and back into the light, was dead.

Sweetie died three months later.

I think about their progeny, and I wish I had kept their line going so I could have a part of Bonk with me today, likely her great, great, great grandchildren. Somewhere, probably in South Florida, Bonk and Sweetie's genes have built a foundation of fiercely loyal, beautiful, transcendent lovebirds. I hope they're cherished as much as I cherished Bonk.

Little Miss Mango, my surviving twin from the single egg from the yellow Fischer's pair I'd had long ago, also lived to be sixteen. I found her dead one morning in her cage, sitting at the front door, waiting to be let out, her head cocked to one side, her eyes half-open. I was heartbroken. I couldn't help but think she had been waiting there for me to soothe her as she took her last breath, but I was absent at her end.

I found Jesse dead at seventeen on the bottom of the cage one morning, and spent several hours crying and pacing my apartment, cradling his body, which was still warm when I found him. He should have survived far longer. Meyer's parrots are known to live upward of thirty years.

I could have ordered a necropsy to determine the cause of death, but one week before he passed, my beloved avian veterinarian, Dr. Z, died suddenly at forty-nine years old. She left behind her husband and two children.

I learned the news through a letter that Dr. Z's veterinary office sent to her patients to tell them that another avian veterinarian would be taking over her practice. I read the letter four times. "Dr. Z" and "passed away" didn't make sense. I spent the next four days in bed. I'd known her twenty years and she was a wellspring of positivity, light, and humor in my world, not to mention great avian and dating advice. Wherever she is, I hope she's flying with the birds. I hope Bonk is with her.

I have not had a drink since that disgusting red beer in Paris on July 9, 2001, and I hope to never have another drink, one day at a time—Poppy would be proud of that, too. Changing my life in that way, breaking the habit, wasn't easy at first, but now drinking is a glimmer of a memory—a bad memory—and I don't want to go back.

I regret not having gone to Poppy's funeral, for not being an adult at twenty-five but rather a sheltered girl who feared retribution and failed to realize her own power. All these years later, I have never been to Poppy's grave. I miss Poppy every day, his advice, his magic tricks, our inside jokes. I still carry a lock of his hair inside *T. S. Eliot's Collected Poems* and I conjure him every time I read "The Love Song of J. Alfred Prufrock":

Do I dare
Disturb the universe?
In a minute there is time
For decisions and revisions which a minute will reverse.

I don't know if I'll ever visit Poppy's cemetery plot. I don't like thinking of him in the ground, only a plaque bearing his name to indicate he was ever here. It's not fair. It disturbs the universe. I know Poppy wouldn't want me sobbing over his grave, dressed in dark colors, neglecting life to mourn him. He'd want me eating banana splits and French fries at Swensen's, laughing with friends, and communing with birds. I think of Poppy when I see pigeons and doves, the harbingers of peace—and I wonder if he's sending them to me, reminding me that where there's life, there's hope—and where there are wings, there is freedom.

Acknowledgments

Thank you to Holt, Gillian Blake, and everyone who worked on this book, especially my patient editor, Barbara Jones, who helped whittle this manuscript into a pleasing bird shape out of an entire unwieldy flock.

I'd like to thank the National Endowment for the Arts, without whom this book would not have been possible.

Thanks to my very first readers for their thoughtful consideration and notes on this story: Tracey Auspitz, Jacqueline Burns, Margaret Finn, Cheryl Fournier, Ramona Hand, Matthew Kurzban, Carol Matthews, Ed Morgan, Saryta Rodriguez, Eleni Russell, Beverly Wixon, and especially fellow South Florida writer Leonard Nash, whose multiple readings and enduring guidance helped both to improve this manuscript and settle my nerves. I can't thank you all enough.

Thank you to Patty Busby, a fellow graduate student at NYU, who said to me, upon hearing my idea for this book and reading a small part of it in workshop: "This isn't just going to be a book about birds. This is a love story between a girl and her grandfather." Your lightbulb moment became the spark that lit this story.

Thank you to my parents for indulging me in birds and allowing me to pursue my avian zeal, despite the noise, chewed furniture, and millet growing out of the carpeting.

Thanks to everyone who appeared in this book—you are the threads that make up the fabric of these pages. Thank you, too, to those outside of these pages who bolstered me through the writing of this book, which was harrowing at times and ecstatic at others.

Finally, with the utmost respect and love, I give a mountain range of gratitude for Joy Tutela, my tenacious and brilliant agent—part disciplinarian, part therapist, part cheerleader—without whom this book would not have wings.

About the Author

Nikki Moustaki is the author of twenty-five books on the care and training of exotic birds. She holds an MA in creative writing, poetry, from New York University, an MFA in creative writing, poetry, from Indiana University, and an MFA in creative writing, fiction, from New York University. She has received a National Endowment for the Arts grant in poetry, as well as many other national writing awards. She splits her time between New York City and Miami Beach. You can find her at www.nikkimoustaki.com.